PRAISE FOR
THE GENEROSITY BET

One of the most important things in our relationship with God is to be charitable with what we steward for Him. Bill High's message isn't just about being generous; it's about the very real process of *becoming* generous. Jesus modeled a life of charity, not just with money but with all that was in Him, and *The Generosity Bet* is an example of the innumerable ways it can take shape. Filled with real-life testimonies about all God has done through obedience in generosity, this book reminds us that God is working in our lives and inspires us to continue in His plan for stewardship.

ROBERT MORRIS
Founding Senior Pastor, Gateway Church
Best-selling author of *The Blessed Life*, *From Dream to Destiny*,
and *The God I Never Knew*

Generosity doesn't come easy for many of us—but we can learn a lot from the examples of others. Bill High has assembled another collection of fascinating accounts from people who have wrestled with the "whys and hows," and discovered God's blessings in the process of living generously.

JIM DALY
President, Focus on the Family

I'm delighted to recommend Bill High's most recent book that leads to discovering the true power of generosity. Undoubtedly, it is an essential message that Americans—and the entire world—must discover. In an age that is driven by self and self-gratification, it's enlightening to read a book that repeatedly demonstrates the best of mankind—serving others through love and generosity.

GOVERNOR MIKE HUCKABEE
Host, "HUCKABEE"

Part of the heritage and legacy of the Maclellan family is our hope to see others give more, and to give more strategically. To this end, *The Generosity Bet* is a fantastic resource that encourages givers to be good stewards of God's resources as they find new and creative ways to give. We are thankful for the work of people like Bill High who are advancing the global generosity movement.

HUGH MACLELLAN JR.
President, The Maclellan Foundation

In *The Generosity Bet* you'll find stories that capture and extend the boundaries of your heart. Sink into the truth about what happens when you give freely to others from all that God has given you. Discover how *impossible* it is for you to make a difference in the lives of others without it making a difference in you. Buy the book and be inspired to begin your own generosity journey.

TAMI HEIM
President and CEO, Christian Leadership Alliance

The Bible is filled with stories of real people with real problems finding real solutions through the reality of their relationship with God. Bill High's new book, *The Generosity Bet*, allows readers to witness God's Word coming alive through the life stories of entrepreneurs and business leaders whose relationship with God has made a real difference. I am inspired as I read these exciting stories. You will be as well!

DR. WILLIAM M. WILSON
President, Oral Roberts University
Empowered21

Bill High has produced a captivating collection of stories that reinforce the connection between generosity and our purpose to glorify God in all that we do. A deep understanding of charity radiates throughout this book and compels readers to look introspectively at their hearts and begin their own journey of generosity.

TONY PERKINS
President, Family Research Council

Often, many Christians are hindered in following the Holy Spirit because of self-imposed limitations. The stories in Bill High's book are examples of how regular people, empowered by the Holy Spirit, live in a way that transforms lives. *The Generosity Bet* is an encouraging word for Christians to be enabled by the Holy Spirit to live a life that truly demonstrates the love of Christ through strategic giving.

HARRY R. JACKSON JR.
Senior Pastor, Hope Christian Church
President, High Impact Leadership Coalition
Presiding Bishop, International Communion of Evangelical Churches

In *The Generosity Bet* Bill High has again captured incredible stories of the Holy Spirit at work in the hearts of generous givers. The stories take us on one inspiring journey after another and are bound to develop better stewards of Kingdom resources!

DAN BUSY
President, Evangelical Council for Financial Accountability

As Joel 2:28 tells us, "And it shall come to pass afterward, that I will pour out My Spirit on all flesh; your sons and your daughters shall prophesy, your old men shall dream dreams, and your young men shall see visions." God is calling us to dream big, and as we hear others' stories, our hearts are impressed by the possibilities for our own lives. As we give expression to those impressions, we're led into a bigger story, one that brings glory to God! We can't hear enough of stories like Bill has captured, and we are very grateful for the individuals who are allowing their stories to be told.

BILL WILLIAMS
CEO, National Christian Foundation

I thought I was a generous giver, but after reading the inspiring stories contained within the pages of *The Generosity Bet*, I was once again challenged to rethink my motives and actions concerning giving. This book has taken me to a new level of generous thinking, and I can't wait to see what the future holds!

BRETT STEPELTON
Trustee and Vice President of Operations,
Festus and Helen Stacy Foundation

An old Hopi Native American proverb says, "He who tells stories, rules the world." Maybe this is true because stories are the most powerful form of communication, and this collection of stories from Bill High is no exception.

DARYL HEALD
Director of Generosity, The Maclellan Foundation

Once again, noted author, speaker, and mentor to leading workplace leaders, Bill High has knocked the ball out of the park within the pages of his new book, *The Generosity Bet*. His excellent storytelling ability shines through the lives of ordinary people who have reached extraordinary success in life while fully committing themselves to faithful generosity. Enjoy this book yourself and then by all means generously share it with everyone you call a friend. In doing so, you may just change their lives forever!

DR. MARK CRESS
Founder, Corporate Chaplains of America

When I read these stories I am struck by the power of one decision. Generous lives don't happen accidentally—they come from an intentional decision to live generously! This book proves it!

BRAD FORMSMA
Creator of ILikeGiving.com
and author of *I Like Giving*

While playing Major League baseball, it was awesome to hit walk-off home runs in front of screaming fans, have my name written in record books, play in All-Star games, and get paid to play a game I would play for free. But as "happy" as these things made me, I only felt joy from my friendship with Jesus as I loved God first and others second. This book shows you the way to a joy-filled life as you give your heart and life to the Giver of all givers.

MIKE SWEENEY
Kansas City Royals

It's been said that reputation is not built on what you are going to do. *The Generosity Bet* shows what happens when ordinary people move past good intentions to a lifestyle of giving where they aim for more than becoming the richest person in the cemetery. These stories challenge us to join an extraordinary God to accomplish the extraordinary.

DAVE DONALDSON
Co-Founder, Convoy of Hope, Inc.

Simple, straightforward, and inspirational, *The Generosity Bet* is packed with wisdom and ideas to spark your own generosity journey. The concept of generosity without a storyline can feel hollow, but Bill High illustrates generosity come to life through compelling narratives about a wide range of people. Well done! Be prepared to be challenged and encouraged at the heart level that giving is indeed a cause greater than ourselves!

TIM SENEFF
President, National Christian Foundation Orlando

All the stories and examples of the people in this book challenged and encouraged me to see what can be done to impact so many lives. In particular, I have watched and experienced firsthand the generosity of Matt McPherson and Bob Hodgdon who wholeheartedly use the generosity of their businesses and lives to reach thousands for the Kingdom. I believe this book will inspire many to join the ranks of those who advance the Gospel message to everyone needing to hear the good news that our Creator is also eager to be our Savior.

GERRY CAILLOUET
Founder and Radio Host, "God's Great Outdoors"

I shared Bill High's last book, *Stories of the Generous Life*, with many of the partners who support Convoy of Hope, Inc. And the response was tremendous. I am confident this book will continue to inspire our partners to an even greater level of generosity. This book is a must-read for every charity.

HAL DONALDSON
President, Convoy of Hope, Inc.

Stories have always been the most powerful tool to encourage and equip believers. Our Savior knew this well as He, through the parables of Scripture we have all come to know and love, shared with us story after story to help us follow Him. The stories contained in this book are real-life journeys of individuals and families seeking first God's Kingdom. As you read them you will see how God has allowed them to experience life that is truly life. The stories in this book will be a tremendous encouragement to all who read them. So grab a cup of coffee, sit back, and travel the road with these folk…you will be glad you did.

DAVID WILLS
President, National Christian Foundation

If there is anyone who's not just an expert on generosity, but has literally lived it out in his own life—in his own family as well as advising many others—it's Bill. I know that the stories, insights, and inspiration contained in *The Generosity Bet* will encourage and challenge many to joyful generosity as they also leave a lasting legacy for their children and families. This thought-provoking book reminds us that while it's easy to talk about generosity, true generosity calls for action in every area of our lives.

CAREY CASEY
CEO, National Center for Fathering

THE
GENEROSITY
BET

THE
GENEROSITY
BET

SECRETS OF RISK,
REWARD, AND REAL JOY

WILLIAM F. HIGH

WITH ASHLEY B. MCCAULEY

DESTINY IMAGE® PUBLISHERS, INC.

P.O. Box 310, Shippensburg, PA 17257-0310

"Promoting Inspired Lives."

This book and all other Destiny Image and Destiny Image Fiction books are available at Christian bookstores and distributors worldwide.

Cover design by: Prodigy Pixel

For more information on foreign distributors, call 717-532-3040.

Or reach us on the Internet: www.destinyimage.com

ISBN 13 TP: 978-0-7684-0701-3

ISBN 13 Ebook: 978-0-7684-0702-0

For Worldwide Distribution, Printed in the U.S.A.

2 3 4 5 6 7 8 / 18 17 16 15

DEDICATION

This book is dedicated to my wife, Brooke. She's been willing to live a great adventure every step of the way—through the good times and the bad times. Every sojourner would be fortunate to have such a faithful companion, friend, and confidante. Most of all, she's the supreme model of generosity through her prayer life, a thousand cold meals while she took care of others, or sharing her dessert with me!

ACKNOWLEDGMENTS

With every work, there are always a thousand acknowledgements that could be delivered. I've been blessed to have the opportunity to work with my daughter, Ashley McCauley, on this project as writer, editor, and creative genius. I'm grateful for the work of Debbie Stacy and her project management skills, as well as the inspiration of my good friend Emmitt Mitchell who has encouraged me to write. I've also been blessed by the Board of Directors of the National Christian Foundation Heartland who have always been willing to take risks and explore new frontiers. I'm also pleased to work with my faithful staff colleagues at National Christian Foundation Heartland who put up with my quirks, new ideas, and quest for the impossible right now. And finally, I'm grateful for the late Pat Lloyd who was willing to dream and believe that we "might change a city."

CONTENTS

FOREWORD by Ron Blue 19

WHY GENEROSITY? 23

INTRODUCTION THE REWARD OF MY GENEROSITY
William F. High, *National Christian Foundation
Heartland* (Olathe, KS) 25

IRRATIONAL GENEROSITY 31

CHAPTER 1 A PASTOR LEARNS IRRATIONAL GENEROSITY
Craig Groeschel, *LifeChurch.tv*
(Edmond, OK) 33

CHAPTER 2 FINDING LIFE AS KINGDOM ENGINEERS
Craig and April Chapman, *INRIX*
(Seattle, WA) 41

CHAPTER 3 BEFORE I REACH THE END OF THE ROAD
Dr. John Koehler, *Physicians Immediate Care*
(Rockford, IL) 49

CAREER GENEROSITY 57

CHAPTER 4 LOGICAL—GIVING AWAY MY BUSINESS
Alan Barnhart, *Barnhart Crane & Rigging*
(Memphis, TN). 59

CHAPTER 5 VENTURES FROM WALL STREET TO ASIA
Henry Kaestner, *Sovereign's Capital*
(Durham, NC) 67

CHAPTER 6   SUPER SERVICE AND HOLY BUSINESS
Dave Lindsey, *DEFENDER Direct*
(Indianapolis, IN) 77

PURPOSEFUL GENEROSITY 85

CHAPTER 7   A THOUSAND LITTLE GIFTS
Rick Warren, *Saddleback Church*
(Lake Forest, CA) 87

CHAPTER 8   CHOOSING DIFFICULT DREAMS
David Hazell, *My Father's World*
(Rolla, MO) 95

CHAPTER 9   THE SHAPE OF MY LIFE AND GOD'S MISSION
Jim Blankemeyer, *MetoKote Corporation*
(Lima, OH) 105

UNCOMFORTABLE GENEROSITY 113

CHAPTER 10   REDISCOVERING THE LOVE OF THE GAME
Jeremy Affeldt, *San Francisco Giants*
(San Francisco, CA) 115

CHAPTER 11   WEALTHY ENOUGH TO FIND PEACE
Vince Elliott, *Financial Advisor*
(Houston, TX) 123

CHAPTER 12   FAITH, FAMILY, AND BASEBALL
Dayton Moore, *Kansas City Royals*
(Kansas City, MO) 133

FAMILY GENEROSITY 139

CHAPTER 13   A PURPOSE FOR THE MERCHANT
David Green, *Hobby Lobby*
(Oklahoma City, OK) 141

CHAPTER 14   BOOKS, BUILDERS, AND OUR 100 PERCENT
Cliff Benson Jr. and Cliff Benson III, *American Homesmith*
(Raleigh, NC) 149

CHAPTER 15   GUNPOWDER AND GENEROSITY
Bob Hodgdon, *Hodgdon Powder Company*
(Shawnee, KS)................................. 157

UNEXPECTED GENEROSITY................................. 165

CHAPTER 16   GIVING CIRCLES AND SEEING MESSY
Anne Irwin, *One Hundred Shares*
(Atlanta, GA) 167

CHAPTER 17   THE WORK OF TRAGEDY, NEED, AND MIRACLES
Debbie Massey and Michelle York, *Helping Hands Ministries*
(Tallulah Falls, GA) 175

CHAPTER 18   A WIDOW'S IDENTITY
Susan Patton, *The Giving Circle*
(Nashville, TN)................................ 183

PERSISTENT GENEROSITY................................. 191

CHAPTER 19   THIS GUITAR-PLAYING ARCHER RUNS
Matt McPherson, *Mathews, Inc.; McPherson Guitars*
(Sparta, WI) 193

CHAPTER 20   RETURN TO EGBE
Don Campion, *Banyan Air Service*
(Fort Lauderdale, FL) 203

CHAPTER 21   A JOURNEY OF SEVEN CAREERS
John and Sherri Kasdorf, *The Kaztex Foundation*
(Pewaukee, WI)................................ 211

GENEROSITY RESOURCES 219

FOREWORD

I was very pleased and privileged to be asked by Bill High to write the foreword for *The Generosity Bet*. I have known Bill for many years and appreciate his passion for generosity, competence as an advisor, and years of experience in helping individuals and families think biblically about money and possessions. We have a kindred spirit when it comes to the practice of generosity.

So why are stories so important? Stories have always had a place in transferring information, knowledge, and wisdom. As Christians, we are all challenged to be salt and light—and what better way do this than to tell real-life stories, my story? Jesus was a storyteller. Think about some of the stories He told: the prodigal son, the Good Samaritan, the parable of the talents, the vineyard owner, etc. We remember those stories and the point being made.

I have been a speaker numerous times at Generous Giving conferences and have heard many great speakers, but what I recall the most are the stories told by real people. In fact, Generous Giving actually did a survey and found that what people most remembered were the stories told at the conferences. While every person's story is unique, they are remembered because stories share themes, principles, and decisions common to everyone.

In my work as a financial counselor, planner, and advisor, I have learned this: God's Word speaks authoritatively and timelessly to all financial planning and decision making. God delights to give principles for the decision being made along with wisdom for the process to walk it out.

Over the years, I have observed that there are two fundamental decisions generous givers make that result in three universally desired consequences. Almost everyone desires 1) contentment regardless of the financial circumstances, 2) confidence in every financial decision, and 3) unparalleled communication between spouses regarding money and money management. Are you interested in these consequences? I know I am. God's Word promises all these things if we follow His principles. The stories you are about to read are examples of these three results. Look for them.

However, there are also two fundamental decisions that are necessary before those three happy results occur. Each person must first decide the answer to these two questions:

- "Who owns it?"

- "How much is enough?"

When I recognize that God owns everything, it changes how I view money. I think and act differently because I am *content* since God is in total control of *His* financial resources. I am *confident* that God knows how to manage *His* money; therefore, my spouse and I are *communicating* about *His* money, not ours. Recognizing this truth changes everything.

The second decision, "How much is enough?" could also be asked as "What is my financial finish line?" or "How much will it take to provide for my needs?" Hebrews 13:5 gives the answer: "Be content with what you have." In other words, if I am not content with what I have, I will never be content with what I don't have.

I recently spoke at a college commencement and closed my talk this way: "If you are dependent on money, you will never have enough. If, on the other hand, you are dependent on God, you will always have enough. The choice is mine, just as it is all of yours."

The stories contained in this great book confirm God's promises. Bill has helped all of us to be encouraged in the faith as we seek God's hand in our own unique journeys. Thank you, Bill.

Ron Blue
Kingdom Advisors
Norcross, GA
May 2014

WHY GENEROSITY?

Therefore, since we are surrounded by so great a cloud of witnesses, let us also lay aside every weight, and sin which clings so closely, and let us run with endurance the race that is set before us, looking to Jesus, the founder and perfecter of our faith, who for the joy that was set before Him endured the cross, despising the shame, and is seated at the right hand of the throne of God.

—HEBREWS 12:1-2

WILLIAM F. HIGH
National Christian Foundation Heartland
(Olathe, KS)

THE REWARD OF MY GENEROSITY

I could sense it in the audience. I was failing. I was trying to connect and somehow persuade them of the power of generosity. But I knew I was somehow missing the mark.

For the past fourteen years, I've been speaking to audiences, both large and small, on the subject of generosity. I've led small groups, preached sermons, and written blogs, articles, and even a book on the subject. And over the past fourteen years, I've had what seems like thousands of meetings with people in coffee shops to discuss this very topic.

But back to my audience and my speaking, I couldn't connect with them for one very simple reason: *I couldn't explain why generosity was important to them.* That experience led me back to the drawing board to ponder, to reflect. Why be generous at all? Why is it important?

WHEN IT'S NOT IN OUR DNA

For the majority of us, generosity is not something we wake up thinking about each day. It's just not in our DNA. If there's any doubt about that, consider two toddlers in a room full of toys. Even though they may have a hundred choices, they will inevitably fight over one toy while staking claim to it with the valiant word of "MINE!" Our very nature seems to crave stuff almost like a security blanket.

So if it's not in our DNA to be generous, why is it so important? I'm at that stage of life where I'm asking myself what it means to be successful. When will I know I have arrived? I'm a driver and a pusher. I like to get things done. I wrestle with contentment. And I have to work at gratitude. But the aching of the human heart is for freedom, grace, and joy.

> The aching of the human heart is
> for freedom, grace, and joy.

SEARCHING FOR SIGNIFICANCE

As I wrestled with these thoughts, I stumbled into a talk by Kevin Myers related to his book *Home Run: Learn God's Game Plan for Life and Leadership*. Kevin talked about how everyone desires a life of significance. Using a baseball metaphor, he said that we run the bases the wrong way: we seek to achieve *significance* by chasing *success* at the cost of the *people* around us and end up with no *self-respect*.

Indeed, there are many great leaders with apparent success—whether business, positional, or power—who have fallen. They spend years seeking to repair the damage done by their relentless pursuit of success at the cost of people and, ultimately, their own character.

And there was my breakthrough. A life of significance can be produced only by a generous life.

Let me explain. Significance is at the core of every human soul. God placed it there. In Ecclesiastes 3:11, the Scripture tells us, "[God] has put eternity into man's heart, yet so that he cannot find out what God has done from the beginning to the end."

This verse tells us two things: First, whether we recognize it or not, it tells us we realize that we are temporary creatures. No matter how much we hit the gym, raid the health food aisle, or manage our stress, not a single one of us can control the number of days we have here on this earth. It's that nagging, gnawing feeling that we are dust in the wind.

But secondly, the verse reminds us of our innate desire to be part of something lasting, something important, something significant. We sometimes refer to it as "the cause greater than ourselves." For ages, men and women have sought to create bridges, museums, libraries, buildings, works of art, and great literature as a means to establishing something lasting. However, significance is only attained through brokenness and surrender—by realizing I cannot build anything on my own that will truly last.

I only attain significance by surrendering to the Creator Christ and realizing that only His work is complete and lasting. To continue to use the baseball metaphor, I begin to run the bases the right way when I surrender to His lordship—to take up my cross daily and follow Him. Then, when I surrender, I can love others in community. Jesus said it this way:

> *A new commandment I give to you, that you love one another: just as I have loved you, you also are to love one another. By this all people will know that you are My disciples, if you have love for one another* (John 13:34-35).

Next, great love is marked by great generosity. As I love others, I will necessarily find myself living generously with all that I am. And a life marked by surrender, love, and generosity is a life that will truly make a difference, a life that is significant.

Great love is marked by great generosity.

To sum it up, we attain significance through surrender, loving others in community, and generosity.

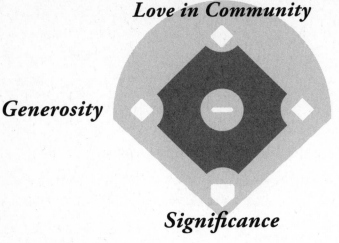

Love in Community

Generosity   *Surrender*

Significance

THE PORTRAIT OF GENEROSITY

As I pondered these things, it occurred to me that I was describing the life of Jesus. Indeed, the most significant life in the whole of human history, the life with the greatest lasting impact, was Jesus's. He was completely surrendered to the will of the Father. He loved His own even to the end. And He gave away His life.

Even as I take a step back and look at the life of Jesus, I see a life of generosity. He stayed late into the night even as people kept bringing Him the sick, the lame, and the demon-possessed to be healed. He defended the adulterous woman about to be stoned. His garment brought healing to the woman who suffered with the flow of blood for twelve long years. He noticed Zacchaeus (and his greater need) in the tree. There always seemed to be an apt word, a timely question, or a piercing challenge. In fact, there were so many acts of generosity that John closes his Gospel with these words:

> *There are so many other things Jesus did. If they were all written down, each of them, one by one, I can't imagine a world big enough to hold such a library of books* (John 21:25 MSG).

What is the impact of a life of generosity? For each of us individually, we experience joy. The writer of Hebrews tells us that Jesus gave away His life "for the joy set before Him." It is not surprising that the same writer tells us to "consider Him" (Hebrews 12:1-2). Each of us is called to consider Jesus as our role model and our example of generosity.

Notably, the concept of generosity Jesus modeled was by no means limited to money. I'm afraid we've allowed the concept of generosity to be narrowed down to the idea of money, giving, tithing, or the latest capital campaign. Jesus taught us that a generous life is so much more. It is a manner of life.

The manner of Jesus's life produced a life of significance, a life of lasting impact. After encouraging us to consider Jesus, the writer of Hebrews tells us that Jesus's life produced a Kingdom that could not be shaken. The description is poetic, if not inspiring:

> But you have come to Mount Zion and to the city of the living God, the heavenly Jerusalem, and to innumerable angels in festal gathering, and to the assembly of the firstborn who are enrolled in heaven, and to God, the judge of all, and to the spirits of the righteous made perfect, and to Jesus, the mediator of a new covenant, and to the sprinkled blood that speaks a better word than the blood of Abel (Hebrews 12:22-24).

So why generosity? Why a life of generosity? The generous life is a life marked by surrender, love in community, and giving away your life. Some of that giving includes money, but many times it does not. The generous life is a life of joy. It's a life of significance—a life of lasting impact.

In the coming pages you'll read the stories of others on their own journey of generosity. None of these people would say they have arrived, but all of them would say they've experienced the same wrestling with the same questions of surrender, significance, gratitude, contentment, and joy.

Read, enjoy, and learn from others along the way.

YOUR STORY:

1. Before reading this introduction, how would you have defined generosity? How has generosity typically been explained to you?

2. What things do people typically pursue in their search for significance or identity? Go back and look at Bill High's baseball diamond illustration on page 28. Do you agree with his statement, "A life of significance can be produced only by a generous life"? Why or why not?

3. Generosity can be difficult to discuss for many reasons: it's hard to define, it's seen as something only feasible for wealthy people, it seems boastful, or we fear what we might be asked to change or give up. What questions or fears do you have about generosity, surrender, significance, gratitude, contentment, or joy?

4. What do you hope to learn from reading these stories?

IRRATIONAL GENEROSITY

We want you to know, brothers, about the grace of God that has been given among the churches of Macedonia, for in a severe test of affliction, their abundance of joy and their extreme poverty have overflowed in a wealth of generosity on their part. For they gave according to their means, as I can testify, and beyond their means, of their own accord, begging us earnestly for the favor of taking part in the relief of the saints—and this, not as we expected, but they gave themselves first to the Lord and then by the will of God to us.

—2 CORINTHIANS 8:1-5

Photo credit: Kayla Thompson

CRAIG GROESCHEL
LifeChurch.tv (Edmond, OK)

CHAPTER 1

A PASTOR LEARNS IRRATIONAL GENEROSITY

Imagine it. Your oil well is about ready to gush and you have the royalties. Not only that, but you're a pastor and this might be your one chance to "cash in." But then someone challenges you: Why don't you give away those royalties?

Craig Groeschel is the pastor of LifeChurch.tv in Edmond, Oklahoma, one of the largest churches in America. Every Sunday on more than nineteen campuses, and more by video, over sixty thousand people hear life-giving messages from God's Word. But, of course, it wasn't always this way.

UNLESS YOU'RE DEBT-FREE...

Craig began the church in 1996 with a handful of people in a two-car garage. After doing market research on non-churchgoers to determine their needs, this church was his response. However, like any new enterprise, finances were thin and unable to stretch as far as their vision.

The concern over financial resources was nothing new for Craig. Growing up, his family instilled a fear of debt and not having enough. He remembers sitting on his grandmother's front porch when he was six or seven and discussing money. As a Depression-era product, his grandmother had never traveled outside of her home state of Texas, and, even at her death in 1994, owned a 1977 Buick with only seventeen thousand miles on it. She told young Craig, "One day the economy will fall apart, and if you're in debt or don't have a lot of money saved, then you won't have anything and won't be able to feed your family."

Another time, his father, who worked in retail, gave him a small gold coin and told him, "One day the economy will collapse, the dollar will be worthless, and if you don't have gold, you won't be able to buy bread." Those two conversations deeply affected him.

On the positive side, those experiences gave Craig a burning desire to succeed along with a commitment to remain debt-free. During high school, he was a standout tennis player and earned a scholarship to Oklahoma City University. In college, Craig's journey was about to take a life-altering turn.

FROM A GIFT TO A CHURCH

While his family attended church, they were not committed to Christ. Like so many young freshmen, Craig joined a fraternity and lived the party scene. He was known as the "wild guy"—the lead party boy. He got into a lot of trouble and guys in his fraternity were even convicted of crimes. In fact, Craig's fraternity was on the verge of being kicked off the campus.

In 1987, in part to rebuff the scrutiny of his fraternity, Craig decided to start a Bible study. Underlying the public relations move, he really wanted to find out more about God. At the time he didn't even have a Bible, but while walking between classes one day a man from the Gideons gave him one.

Craig began reading the New Testament, and when he got to Ephesians 2 he read about the grace of God for the first time and committed his life to Christ. His life was transformed—he went from being known as the party guy to the Bible study guy. Eventually, the Bible study he led grew so large that they had to move into a church.

From there, Craig felt called to the ministry, but he had a business degree, so he took a commercial job. In 1991, the same year he married Amy, Craig's pastor told him that if he could get forty young people to join the church, they would hire him. With that goal in mind, Craig quickly found the people and was hired. However, he was still a long way from giving generously.

Craig heard his first message on tithing when he was nineteen—not long after he'd received Christ. As a result, he wrote out his first tithe check. The same day, his grandmother (the same one who warned him about the economy collapsing and who didn't appear to have any money) called Craig and asked if she could give him money so he could buy himself a car. Craig thought, "Wow, this giving stuff really works!" Yet, in those early days, Craig would tell you his tithing was more about obedience and duty—not joy.

In 1996, Craig started Life Church. He and Amy put everything they had into the church to get it started. At one level, it was one of his first generous acts, but Craig said, "In other ways, it was kind of selfish, because the church was something I was doing. It felt generous at the time, but it was still investing in the Kingdom I believed in." They also started giving more than a tithe at that time—10 percent to the church, 10 percent to the building, and occasional gifts to help people in need.

THE OPPORTUNITY

Around that time, God began working on him—through his wife, Amy. She always wanted to give and encouraged him to give more. He knew there was a sense that he was putting his trust in what he had rather than in God. But the defining moment was soon to come.

By 2005, the church had grown so much that people were beginning to request his sermons and were willing to pay money to get them. The church investigated the proper way to handle this issue. As the pastor, Craig would own the rights to the sermons and receive royalties from their sales. The opportunity for income was significant.

In a meeting to discuss what to do with the sermons, one of his fellow pastors, Bobby Gruenewald, asked, "What would happen if we just gave them away?" The silence was stunning. Why would anyone suggest he give away something of so much value to him? The ship had come home. The opportunity was there.

What would happen if we just gave them away?

In that moment, Craig felt like the Holy Spirit breathed upon him: *this was the right thing to do—just give them away.* He said, "My only real hesitation was not actually that I wouldn't get the money, but what if we couldn't afford to keep giving the sermons away? As a church, we did not have extra at that time—we were actually at the peak of our debt."

Craig continued, "That moment changed us—the church and I. Generosity became one of my top values." For the first time, he was giving away something of great value to him and he was giving to people who would never give back. "It was a pure gift," he said.

From that moment on, giving became contagious. It began to penetrate every corner of their church. As they developed resources, it became standard to just give them away. Generosity became a value. As Craig said, "Generosity is not something we do—it is something we are."

Generosity is not something we do— it is something we are.

Today, they've given away more than five million resources to over one hundred ten thousand church leaders. In addition to sermons and teaching, they've given away everything from kid's curriculums to church management systems. The church has more than one hundred seventy-five to two hundred network churches as well. These churches use Life Church's sermon resources and kids' curriculum every week, but none of these churches count as part of Life Church's congregation, nor is an affiliation fee charged. Also, Craig will tell you they've never attempted to quantify any of these efforts; it's all been a gift.

One of their most significant gifts has been YouVersion, the world's most popular Bible application with more than 150 million downloads around the world. To date, Life Church has given more than $30 million to this project that is run by twenty-nine full-time staff members. The gift of the Bible hearkens back to Craig's days in college when a Gideon New Testament was handed to him and changed his life.

HOW GENEROSITY DEFINES LIVES

Today, Craig and Amy live on a fraction of what they make. Their six children have gotten into the act as well. If anything, their younger children are "too generous" with a tendency to give everything away. "We've got to teach them some habits of saving and investing," Craig said. But as a family, they've seen how giving has impacted every area of their lives—including other people who have joined them in their own giving.

Not long ago, Craig decided to fulfill one of his wife's dreams—helping women in crisis who have left safe homes but need a transitional living space as they return to the world. For months, Craig and Amy looked for the right house, but could not find anything that fit. They decided to place the desire on hold. Then they got a call out of the blue from a pastor friend who wanted to show them a house—even though they had never told anyone about their plans. When they got to the house, it was perfect—fully remodeled, fully furnished—everything was exactly as they would have done.

The woman who owned the house attended their church. She told Craig and Amy she had purchased the house to flip, but God put it on her heart that Amy was supposed to use it to help women. She was willing to rent it to them for her costs of $900 per month. Craig noted that the house was easily worth $2,000 per month. However, within two weeks, the woman called back and said, "I cannot do this. I simply cannot do this! I need to *give* this house to your ministry." Craig told a shortened version of this story in church and another family stepped up and offered a house as well.

That's the crazy life of generosity—as Craig and Amy have learned. The defining moment of learning to give even when it doesn't make sense changed their lives. It has defined them as individuals and it's defined their church. Today, one of the tenets of their church reads as follows: "We will lead the way with irrational generosity because we truly believe it is more blessed to give than to receive."

YOUR STORY:

1. What early influences shaped your thoughts about saving, spending, and giving? How have those moments or lessons influenced how you handle your finances today?

2. Craig experienced a turning point in his own giving journey when he gave away something of value to him and could not be repaid. What turning points have you experienced in your own journey?

3. What allows people to get to a place where they can be "irrational" in their giving?

GENEROSITY

CRAIG AND APRIL CHAPMAN
INRIX (Seattle, WA)

CHAPTER 2

FINDING LIFE AS KINGDOM ENGINEERS

Craig and April Chapman are engineers. As such, they like having life mapped out, a blueprint to follow, an order to things. But sometimes God has different plans. Craig and April will be the first to tell you their journey has not been what they would have scripted. April became a Christian in high school, and Craig in college. Despite their early faith, they each went through a divorce. In 1994, when they married, they each brought significant debt into the marriage.

FIRST STEPS

Growing up, Craig and April were taught the importance of hard work, responsibility, and financial independence—but not generosity. They learned their lessons well: both were honor students, attended college, and started well-paying careers in software engineering.

The first step in their generosity journey together came when April was introduced to Malachi 3:10. She shared with Craig that it is the only place in Scripture where God asks people to test Him:

Bring the full tithe into the storehouse, that there may be food in My house. And thereby put Me to the test, says the Lord of hosts, if I will not open the windows of heaven for you and pour down for you a blessing until there is no more need.

Malachi 3:10 is the only place in Scripture where God asks people to test Him.

Confronted with this truth from Scripture, they took the first step of tithing. Craig said, "I knew about the tithe before, but I had assumed it was Old Testament law that didn't apply since we placed our trust in Jesus. Now, we both knew that if we truly loved God, we needed to obey His command to give a minimum of ten percent." God was true to His Word and the Chapmans saw their income increase and their debt go down.

In addition to the challenge from Scripture, they read the autobiography of R. G. LeTourneau, a prolific giver, a businessman with over three hundred patents, and the founder of LeTourneau University. They followed LeTourneau's example of increasing their giving percentage every year, a habit that prepared their hearts for additional giving opportunities.

NEXT STEPS: UNDERSTANDING LIFE

After Craig and April married, they moved from California to Washington where they both worked for Microsoft. This was during the 1990s, the "boom years" for Microsoft, and they received stock options that quickly appreciated in value. Starting in 1999, they began cashing in their shares and converting them to other investments as part of a diversification strategy. This strategy of cashing in stock options allowed them to significantly increase their giving.

At a donor conference in Colorado, God chose to speak more directly to them than He ever had before. "We both felt a tangible message that

He had a plan for us that would shake up our status quo and direct the next period of our lives," Craig said. Shaking up the status quo can be a scary thing for engineers, but they both had the sense that God was directing them away from Microsoft and into service for Him.

The Chapmans questioned this calling: How could they serve God? "We were technology geeks," Craig said, "and we had none of the 'special' skills we expected for those in Christ-centered ministry."

> We had none of the "special" skills we expected
> for those in Christ-centered ministry.

Soon after the Colorado event, they attended a Campus Crusade conference where they learned an acronym that became part of the next step in their journey. They discovered they should use their LIFE—Labor, Influence, Finances, and Expertise—to serve Christ.

With this in mind, April left Microsoft in early 2000 and began serving Christ-centered organizations with her gift: Internet strategy consulting. It was also an exciting time as they celebrated the birth of their twins, a boy and a girl.

SIGNIFICANCE IN CHRIST

In 2003, Craig left Microsoft to join April in ministry work. At first, he worried about losing his sense of identity and value that comes from work. However, he had just read Bob Buford's book *Halftime* and realized he was in a new chapter of his life. More importantly, he realized his significance was in Christ—not his career. Craig was soon to learn that "ministry work" can show up in different forms.

In early 2004, Craig began talking to a friend who wanted to start what would become INRIX, a traffic and navigation company. He seriously resisted the opportunity at first, believing that his job was now full-time Kingdom ministry. However, during one of Craig's quiet times, God told him to join the start-up. At the exact moment God gave Craig the vision for the company, the phone rang. It was Craig's business partner asking for an answer because he was filing the company's incorporation papers. Craig said, "It just blew me away because the moment my partner called for the answer, God had just given me the answer."

God gave Craig two caveats with this decision: Build a company that emphasizes integrity and family values (not always easy for a technology company), and plan on giving away half of anything he made from his equity in INRIX.

INRIX became a successful company during Craig's time there. Although his plan was to stay at the job for about two years, it was seven before he felt released to return to full-time ministry.

Shortly before Craig left INRIX, a new investor offered to divest Craig of some of his INRIX equity, a deal that would allow Craig to pursue full-time ministry and fulfill his promise to give away 50 percent of his equity. However, when Craig left in June 2011, the deal had still not materialized. "I had made a promise to be generous," Craig said, "but now I was dependent entirely on God to make this plan work. I had to learn to trust because I was kind of a basket case."

"He was hard to live with," April agreed.

Finally, on August 22, 2011, an email hit Craig's inbox telling him that the deal would close. It was the fulfillment of his commitment to give away 50 percent of his equity. Now both Chapmans had the flexibility to fully devote their time to Kingdom service.

Looking back, April said, "If Craig had not been obedient to join INRIX, we would have missed all the blessings and impact God is allowing us to have now. Through INRIX, Craig gained another set of skills that now drives one of our passions—innovation. And while we love what we are doing, we are actively seeking the Lord to make sure we don't miss any other big adventures He might have planned."

The Journey Continues

Today, the Chapmans are involved in many ministries at a donor, board, and service level where they focus on technology, innovation, Christian leadership, and marriage and family. April said, "We like to model our ministry involvement after Acts 1:8 where Jesus talks about going to Jerusalem, Judea, Samaria, and the ends of the earth. We try to serve local, regional, national, and international ministries to help ensure we're loving all of our neighbors."

The Chapmans know they still have more lessons to learn on their generosity journey. Last year, they took a trip to the Dominican Republic and Zambia with World Vision. "We're recognizing the conflict you can feel in the First World when you have a heart for God and want to love people well," April said. "We spent some time with joyful brothers and sisters in Zambia who have nothing, and then we came back to a home remodel where we were making choices about light fixtures and carpeting. There's a healthy tension that is making us think."

Craig added, "I think we've realized it all belongs to God, but how much is enough? Is there a financial finish line or is the goal to accumulate more? I think God is fine with us having a comfortable lifestyle, but there is a point where we should stop trying to accumulate and start finding more ways to serve and give away our resources."

> One thing we're finding is that everyone's journey is unique.

April concluded, "One thing we're finding is that everyone's journey is unique. It's not prescriptive. What God has shown us, or what He has done in our lives, is not exactly what He's going to do in others. The opportunities He's given us are unique to the skills He's given us. If there's any common thread, it's that we have to be available, be seeking Him, and be asking Him to show us opportunities. Then, we have to obey."

"Too many people look at generosity stories and think, 'I can't do that,'" Craig said. "Even I listen to many of the Generous Giving stories and feel like the rich man in the Bible who had to walk away. I think, 'Man, I can't do that.' But God doesn't necessarily want that from me. Maybe that's not what God is calling me to. But I do have be asking, 'What *is* God calling me to?'"

YOUR STORY:

1. At first, Craig thought tithing was not applicable because it's an Old Testament concept; however, a key verse that sparked the Chapman's generosity journey was Malachi 3:10. Research and write down several verses about giving from both the Old and New Testaments that speak to your spirit.

2. Craig and April use what many might term their "secular" (non-ministry) skills in software development and Internet strategy for Kingdom purposes. If you're a layperson, how can you use your LIFE (Labor, Influence, Finances, and Expertise) in creative ways to serve God? If you're in the ministry world, how can you encourage laypeople that their skills matter, and challenge them to use them?

3. Sometimes we have good opportunities to serve God, like Craig did when he first left Microsoft to join April in serving ministries. However, God called Craig back to the business world because He had another plan. How are you practicing listening to God now so you'll know the sound of His voice when moments like these occur?

4. The Chapmans pointed out that everyone has a unique journey and is called to give and serve in different ways. If you're feeling overwhelmed by these giving stories, stop. Realize you might not be called to do everything others have done. Instead, take some time today and over the next weeks and months to pray about where God is specifically calling you.

GENEROSITY

DR. JOHN AND DENA KOEHLER

DR. JOHN KOEHLER
Physicians Immediate Care
(Rockford, IL)

CHAPTER 3

BEFORE I REACH THE END OF THE ROAD

At the beginning, Dr. John Koehler had no grand plans of creating his own business or making money; he just wanted to solve a problem. Some ten to fifteen years later—and now as the owner of a prosperous network of urgent care clinics—he was at a conference in the Bahamas where many senior businessmen talked about generosity. He assumed he was off the hook because of his youth and relative lack of wealth—he would give later, when he had their level of resources.

QUESTIONS AND OPPORTUNITIES

When John was young, he lived in Africa for five years where his father was a church planter before political instability necessitated their return to the States. He spent the remainder of his childhood in a small town in Pennsylvania where his father pastored a church. He attended Wheaton College, where he met his wife, Dena, before going on to Penn State for medical school.

While John completed his residency in emergency medicine in Grand Rapids, he noticed it had over ten urgent care clinics, which is a lot for one city. John moved to his wife's hometown of Rockford, Illinois, and began working in a hospital emergency room. One day he asked his wife, "Where are all the urgent care clinics?"

She responded, "I don't believe we have any."

John saw his opportunity and began talking with several of his ER partners. "You need something in between the family doctors/pediatricians and the ER," he said. "Urgent care has long hours and you can walk right in. It has the access of the ER with less wait time at one-fifth of the cost."

Along with his ER partners, John found a building that was actually built for urgent care, but no hospital wanted it. About seven months later, in April 1987, they opened Physicians Immediate Care, their first urgent care center. "You'll find most entrepreneurs have a genetic predisposition that when they see an opportunity, they have a difficult time resisting the urge to capitalize on that opportunity," John said. "I had no clue about starting a business or running it; I just made an observation to my wife that there were no urgent care centers here."

A STORY OF GROWTH

Within a year and a half, John opened a second clinic after they outgrew the first. However, between 1989 and 1990, through a series of circumstances where a prospective partner reneged on a deal, they went from two prosperous clinics to two clinics on the verge of bankruptcy. In order to meet payroll, John had to borrow $50,000 from his grandmother. Even in the midst of all of this, John and Dena never stopped giving to any of the missionaries they supported.

Through the grace of God, the company survived and went on to build twenty clinics with an additional nine gained through a private equity transaction in July 2012. Today, they have thirty clinics in three states and are continuing to expand. They are the number one urgent care provider in the Midwest and the ninth largest provider in the country.

As their urgent care centers grew, so did their needs, many of which were unique to urgent care. So John began starting companies whenever they encountered a problem without a good solution. Today, Practice Velocity provides electronic medical records along with billing and database software solutions for urgent care centers. They also have Urgent Care Alliance, a purchasing organization; Urgent Care Assurance Company, a medical malpractice company; and the Urgent Care Association of America, a trade association they co-founded.

"We just kept following our noses and asking, 'God, should we do this?'" John said. "And I felt God saying, 'Go into the land. I'm going to bless you.' And He did."

ENTERING THE GIVING PARADIGM

Giving has always been part of John's life, as shown by his commitment to support missionaries even when his company was almost bankrupt. As a child, he faithfully tithed on whatever he earned when he mowed lawns or trapped animals for fur.

When John was in his early forties, he and Dena attended a conference at a Bahamian resort where they heard the generosity stories of a number of senior businessmen. John said, "I was probably forty-two years old and there were guys with gray and silver hair talking about giving to the Lord's work and how the Lord had blessed them. I'm thinking, 'Yeah, this is great! I'm glad for these guys. Of course, this doesn't really apply to me. I'm too young and I don't have much money now.' At the time, I was just building clinics and putting all the money back into the business."

Then another speaker stood up. Scott Lewis was John's age, maybe younger. "Scott started talking about giving one million [dollars] to Campus Crusade over several years with a little machine shop company he has," John said. "One year, Scott didn't have money to give and told his wife they needed to use what they did have to meet payroll. His wife responded, 'I'll write the [donation] check if you don't.' Another year, they had the 'Closed' sign on the company door, but decided to switch it to 'Open.' That day, they made twenty-seven thousand dollars in profits that made the difference. It was miraculous."

As John sat there, the Lord worked on his heart through Scott's testimony. After the conference, John went to write a $10,000 check. Pulling out his checkbook was one of the most difficult things he had ever done. "I could hardly write it," John said. "It was really hard for me to give away that much money in one big chunk. Normally we'd give something like five hundred bucks, which is a lot of money, but this was ten thousand dollars."

But as soon as John wrote the check, he was released. "Amazing!" John said. "I call it the giving paradigm. When I wrote that check, I entered the giving paradigm and the Lord put a desire in my heart to make money and give it away. Through Scott Lewis's testimony, and then a big check, the Lord came in and changed my heart to a different paradigm."

> When I wrote that check, I entered the giving paradigm.

He continued, "We need to enter the giving paradigm to experience greater joy in giving, greater purpose in God's work. You can have a paradigm of generosity when you tithe, or even when you give fifteen percent and feel like you're really rocking it, but that's not how it works. The Lord wants all of it. He wants one hundred percent, not just ten or fifteen percent."

POSSESSIONS AND OUR CHILDREN'S INHERITANCE

When John and Dena returned from the conference, they called a family meeting in the living room. They had heard horror stories about children suing their Christian parents for giving away "too much" money, so they wanted to proactively address their children's financial expectations. They told their children, "Don't expect much of an inheritance from us. We will pay for your education and help you through, and there might be other things we can help you with, but don't count on a large inheritance from us because it's being given away to the Lord's work."

John's children know their parents are completely unified in their giving habits and goals. John and Dena don't share numbers with their children, but their kids know it's a lot of money. "Kids are good observers," John said. "They see what you're doing. They see we don't have big cars, own second homes, or go on fancy vacations. I've also told my family I'm staying away from toys. I don't want toys because they just kill you because of the work involved! So where is all the money going? Well, to the Lord's work."

However, John believes in having savings and providing for his family: "We do save for our retirement assets and our kids' education, but we're not tempted to accumulate stuff. And our kids do have a good life—our house is plenty big and there's never been any lack. All eight of our children (ages fourteen to twenty-nine) love to be home for the holidays. Everyone gets along with everyone and there are no big rifts in our family, which is a gift."

GIVING METHODS, ASIA, AND CHICKENS

John and Dena have several giving vehicles, including a giving fund that has been financed in part through company stock donations and the recapitalization of their business. They do not have an exact giving method, but tend to find new ministries through the "Ping-Pong effect"—friends' recommendations or other ministry connections.

Much of their giving is done in Southeast Asia because John and Dena go on a medical missions trip to Thailand every year. There they support Faith Comes by Hearing Bible listening programs and language translation work along with other ministries involved in transmitting short-wave Christian radio programs, rescuing girls from the sex industry in Chiang Mai, offering interest-free micro-development loans, or supporting widows.

One of John's favorite stories is when they began supporting widows in Laos. They sent money, via local pastors, so widows could purchase chickens and support themselves by selling chicks and eggs. However, John told the pastors that when they gave the money to the women, they were to say, "You have not gone unnoticed. There's a God in Heaven who loves you and this came from Him." Later, one of the pastors returned to a village to visit the widows. They proudly showed him their chickens and said, "These are God's chickens."

These are God's chickens.

"I like how that translated in their minds," John said. "It's not just that some American gave money, but God saw them and provided for them, so these were God's chickens." Today, John and Dena help the Circle of Love Foundation support two hundred thirty-one widows with the goal of someday supporting one thousand. The Koehlers also keep a book that has a photo of each of the women they help support.

GIVE AS YOU GO

When John thinks about advice he would give, especially to younger people, he said, "You absolutely must give as you go. You have to do that. Don't think, 'I'll give in five years; I'll give in ten years; I'll give when I retire.' If your investments go up in flames, you lose that money and you lose the ability to give. You lose the opportunity to enter the giving paradigm. You absolutely must give as you go.

"You never know when the tide will turn for better or worse: If the Lord brings in a huge return after twenty years of business, then great, you gave for twenty years and you can continue to give more. But if you built a business and then went bankrupt after twenty years, you'll be glad you gave as you went and supported a lot of missions work before running out of money.

"I've seen too many people who hoarded money, then made a big business venture thinking they'd get more and, therefore, could give more later. But then they went bankrupt. And they never gave. They worked their entire career, their whole lives, and they never gave. *They never gave!* I wouldn't want to go to my grave with that. You don't want to be at the end of the road and handing off the baton to the next generation and you never gave. Don't miss out on the joy of generosity. It's a wonderful gift to be able to give and to have that joy."

YOUR STORY:

1. John, and the man who influenced him, Scott Lewis, entered the giving paradigm by giving away a large sum of money. While God does not call everyone to this, could writing a large check be God's way of helping your heart let go of whatever you are holding on to? (Scott's story is featured in the 2013 book *Stories of the Generous Life* in the chapter "From Scam Artist to Million-Dollar Miracle.")

2. John and Dena have already communicated their financial expectations to their children and are choosing not to leave a large inheritance. What is the balance between giving everything and leaving finances or possessions to your heirs? How are you communicating this to your children now?

3. When John gave money so Laotian widows could buy chickens, what influenced the women most was the message he sent: "You have not gone unnoticed. There's a God in Heaven who loves you." How can the message of your gift also be used to change people's lives and bring glory to God?

4. John's advice is to "give as you go" because you don't know how long you will have the opportunity and ability to be generous. What fears, concerns, desires, or other issues are holding you back from giving now?

CAREER GENEROSITY

If you make $22,000 a year, you are in the wealthiest 9.7 percent of the world.

—World Wealth Calculator

As for the rich in this present age, charge them not to be haughty, nor to set their hopes on the uncertainty of riches, but on God, who richly provides us with everything to enjoy. They are to do good, to be rich in good works, to be generous and ready to share, thus storing up treasure for themselves as a good foundation for the future, so that they may take hold of that which is truly life.

—1 Timothy 6:17-19

GENEROSITY

ALAN BARNHART
Barnhart Crane & Rigging
(Memphis, TN)

CHAPTER 4

LOGICAL—GIVING AWAY MY BUSINESS

For many people, life is a series of events occurring by default. But for a few, life is made of intentional decisions to respond to God's Word and His Spirit. For Alan Barnhart, once he came to know the person of Christ and began to study God's Word, it was only logical that he would give away his business.

Alan is the CEO of Barnhart Crane & Rigging. And if you like toys—really big toys—then you'd love Barnhart Crane & Rigging. The company picks up and transports heavy objects—things like wind turbines and parts for nuclear power plants. More recently, the company was selected to move the world's largest tunnel boring machine to Seattle. Like a large drill bit, the machine was five stories high and weighed seven thousand tons. If you've got something really big to move, chances are you will call Barnhart Crane.

It doesn't take long to see that Alan really loves his work. But there's a backstory too—long before the company ever became "successful" and profitable, Alan made a decision about how he would handle wealth.

SEEING THE WORLD DIFFERENTLY

When he was eight, Alan began working in the family business that operated out of his parents' home. Throughout high school and college, he and his brother, Eric, worked as crane operators and metal workers.

While Alan's family attended a Methodist church, it was not until tenth grade that Alan understood the Gospel when he began attending his school's Young Life program. That summer, he went to a Young Life camp and accepted Christ. Not much about his life changed until the following summer when he returned to the camp as part of the work crew. "That was a life changer for me because for the first time in my life, I was around a bunch of people my age who were living their faith," Alan said. "When I came back my senior year, I lived very differently."

After high school, Alan studied civil engineering at the University of Tennessee. While people often fall away from faith during college, Alan grew tremendously in his Christian walk as he got involved with Young Life and InterVarsity campus ministries.

Halfway through his senior year of college, Alan began learning more about world hunger as he read *Rich Christians in an Age of Hunger* by Ron Snyder and participated in a World Vision 30-Hour Famine. In particular, Alan and his roommate began wrestling with the famine occurring in Ethiopia at the time. They donated $350—the money they had saved for a spring break ski trip to Colorado—and spent their break at a local lake. Alan said, "I know my three hundred fifty dollars didn't change much about Ethiopia, but it changed me. It was a turning point in my life that gave me a heart for the poor."

My $350 didn't change much about
Ethiopia, but it changed me.

After Alan graduated from college, some friends advised him to do something significant with his life—go to seminary or join the Young Life staff. But Alan felt God had gifted him in construction, so he returned to his own mission field—the family business.

In his first two years out of college, Alan studied every verse in the Bible related to wealth and finances, wrote them all down, and catalogued them. Through that study, he developed a healthy sense of fear of the possible effects of affluence. "Now, I'm not a guy given to irrational fears," Alan said. "My wife and co-workers would probably say I could use a little more fear, but this isn't an irrational fear—the Scripture is full of warnings about wealth."

A key verse for Alan was Luke 12:15, "And [Jesus] said to them, 'Take care, and be on your guard against all covetousness, for one's life does not consist in the abundance of his possessions.'" In that passage, Jesus told a parable about the man who filled up his barns and built bigger barns so he could house even more. "I'm sure his neighbors thought he was a success," Alan said. "But at the end, God said to him, 'You fool. You got it wrong. You lived your entire life with one paradigm, but the paradigm was wrong and it led to your destruction.' God said this is how it will be with anyone who stores up things for himself and is not rich toward God."

WHEN SUCCESS COULD BE SPIRITUAL FAILURE

Shortly after Alan got engaged to Katherine, a young woman he met his senior year of college, the couple attended the 1984 Urbana conference. There they heard about the need overseas, tentmaker missionaries, and how engineers had access to closed countries. They decided to become missionaries to Saudi Arabia for at least a few years. Katherine was especially excited because she had always dreamed of being a missionary.

But as Alan and Katherine prepared to go overseas just months after their wedding, Alan's parents approached him: they were retiring and were going to spend the next year sailing around the world. If Alan and his brother wanted the company, they could have it; otherwise, Alan's parents would sell it.

At first, there was no unity about their decision or even which direction they should take. Alan's brother, Eric, said he would take his half of the business and Alan could use his own half however he liked. Then Alan felt like he needed to join the business with Eric, but Katherine wanted to be a missionary. Alan said, "Katherine and I kept voting, but it kept being one to one. Finally Katherine said, 'I'll submit to you, but I think you're wrong, you're probably going to fail, get swallowed by a whale, and then we can go to the mission field.'"

However, even though Alan wanted to go into business, he looked at it as a dangerous thing if they succeeded. He and Eric were acutely aware that "earthly success could be spiritual failure." Before they made any money from the company, they decided to set a financial finish line—a middle-class salary they would not exceed even if the business prospered.

One evening, Alan, Eric, and their wives gathered to pray, entrust the business to God, and commit to a financial finish line. After that meeting, Alan finally had peace about the direction they were going together. And while they made their commitment before the Lord to not store up wealth, Alan and Eric told a few friends and some people at the company about it. "That locked in our decision and gave us some real accountability," Alan said. "We set out not to get rich. We set out to *avoid* being rich."

> We set out not to get rich.
> We set out to **avoid** being rich.

Since the brothers took over the company, it has grown tremendously, usually at about 25 percent every year. Today, Alan draws his finish line salary of $125,000 from the company that has $250 million in annual revenue with nine hundred employees in twenty locations around the United States.

Alan also still loves his job. "I don't see running the business as a distraction from my ministry; it is my ministry. When financials come out, I'm very interested to see what we're doing and if we're making money. Some people might look askance at that, but I don't—it's just part of restoring order to our part of creation. I want to push hard, be good at it, and work according to scriptural principles."

HOW TO GIVE AWAY A BUSINESS

As the company continued to grow, especially in their capital-rich business, it became worth hundreds of millions of dollars. "There's a lot of hassle associated with something that valuable, especially as you try to figure out what happens if someone dies," Alan said. "We were spending a lot of time and money trying to figure out what to do. But then we said, 'This is God's money. We shouldn't be spending this time and money trying to figure out what to do. Instead, we should give it away.'" The financial advisors they met with called them crazy and said it was ridiculous to think of giving away a company.

Shortly after, they found the National Christian Foundation who walked them through the process of donating their ownership in the company to a giving fund. "We gave away ninety-nine percent of the company while still maintaining control. So we transferred the *value* of the company without transferring the *stewardship*. The value has so much danger, but the stewardship has so much power. The company can continue to be a ministry-funding tool for years to come."

Even though some people have told Alan he is insane for giving away the company, he said it makes sense to him: "I think it's perfectly logical. The day we made the transfer, my balance sheet changed a lot, but my life didn't change at all. I'm convinced it's much more fun to be a giver than a consumer."

He continued, "When people stop to examine the stuff they're buying, oftentimes they'll find their mindset is negative. They've reached their goals, but their goals are not ones that lead to life and fulfillment. But a lot of people don't stop to examine their motives. The river is flowing in one direction, and if you don't do some intentional paddling, you'll tend to go the same direction our whole society is flowing."

THE FOUR BENEFITS

Through his giving journey, Alan has seen four benefits of generosity: First, there is an abundant life that comes when God blesses people for living His life. Second, Alan and his family have developed relationships with brothers and sisters around the world as they have traveled to over fifty countries and seen what God is doing worldwide. They do 90 percent of their giving internationally because that is where they see a disproportionate need. The third benefit is freedom from fear. There is relief in knowing that because God owns it all, they can hold everything with an open hand.

Finally, there is a huge benefit in raising children. Alan's children have the benefit of not growing up as the "rich kids." In addition, his children have been able to travel the world, see various ministries, and sit at the dinner table with many different people. Through these experiences, their perspectives have been broadened.

However, Alan and Katherine do want to leave something behind for their children: "We believe in leaving our kids a rich inheritance," Alan said, "and we are trying to do that, but we think it has very little to do with money. In fact, most often it's counterproductive to leave them money. But we do want to leave them a rich inheritance."

In conclusion, Alan said, "We can get enamored with stories of generosity that have lots of numbers and zeroes. I don't think that's the point. There are plenty of people who have gone down this path of generosity who are smarter, godlier, and more faithful, and the outcome has looked very different externally. Don't get caught up with the numbers, but with the concept of freedom. Start wherever you are, with whatever you have. The life of a steward is a great way to live."

YOUR STORY:

1. One of Alan's first sacrificial gifts was using his spring break trip money for famine relief. Often, generosity begins with little gifts like these. What small step can you take today to say yes to God's invitation to join Him on the generosity journey?

2. Alan's early study of every Bible verse about wealth was very influential in his life. Some of his favorite passages are Malachi 3:8-12, Luke 12:15-21, 1 Timothy 6:6-10, and James 5:1-6.   Read the above verses and spend some time reflecting on them. How did you hear God through those verses?

3. Alan believed that business success could be dangerous to their family if they weren't prepared to handle it well and be accountable to others. What commitments have you made to ensure success will be a positive thing for your family? Who is holding you accountable to those standards?

4. Alan said it is important for people to stop and examine their motives as they purchase items or make financial goals. Take a moment to think about your last purchase and your financial objectives. What motivated those decisions? How are you being intentional about creating goals that lead to life and true joy?

HENRY KAESTNER
Sovereign's Capital (Durham, NC)

GENEROSITY

CHAPTER 5

VENTURES FROM WALL STREET TO ASIA

Henry's story might sound like a crazy California surfer story if he didn't happen to be from the East Coast. But that's what his story has been—a wild ride. No one would fund the first two of Henry's business ventures. While they seemed like good ideas, investors thought there was just too much risk. Looking back, even Henry said he wouldn't have funded them himself. However, both companies are now multi-million dollar enterprises that span Henry's faith and generosity journeys.

FIRST VENTURES

Henry grew up in Baltimore, Maryland, with the last vestiges of wealth. Several generations ago, both sides of his family had been very wealthy; however, it had dissipated by his parents' generations. Yet as he was exposed to wealth through relatives who directly inherited the family money, it attracted him. He said, "I always saw wealth from afar. That definitely was a big driver for me growing up."

After graduating from the University of Delaware with a degree in international relations, Henry started several companies, but had to dissolve them after running into copyright issues. After a brief stint at a major accounting firm, he moved over to Wall Street. There he and a group of institutional brokers decided to start their own firm. Each person in the group was needed to establish the market coverage required for the new company's survival, but one by one, each person backed out after evaluating the risks. The last two were Henry's closest friends in the industry—they would later die in the September 11th terrorist attacks at the desk he once shared with them.

Undaunted, Henry moved to North Carolina in 1997 where he could afford to hire people to replace those who had backed out. Henry attempted to raise capital for his firm, Chapel Hill Brokers, but he did not receive any. "Looking back, I know why nobody would fund me," Henry said. "It made no sense. I wouldn't have funded me."

Instead, Henry took out a series of credit cards and immediately maxed them out. Several times he came close to losing everything—sometimes he was only one day away from having to fold and let go of everyone. However, everything came together and they became the country's number one ranked broker of electricity derivatives. At their peak, they were transacting more than $150 million a day. In 2000, Henry sold Chapel Hill to APB Energy, which became the energy broking arm of ICAP, the largest broker of derivatives in the world.

ONE OF *THOSE* CHURCHES

Despite having so much financial success, Henry had an incredible amount of anxiety. He should have been content, but something was missing. The search for the answer began shortly after moving to North Carolina in 1997. Henry and Kimberley, his then-girlfriend (now wife), had grown up in a culture that said if you wanted to get into a social circle where people were generally moral and nice, you went to church. So they visited a number of churches, one of which was a conservative church that preached the Gospel. At first, they were taken aback because it was one of *those* "born-again" churches, but they continued to visit.

It was one of **those** "born-again" churches, but they continued to visit.

Henry had grown up attending a liberal church where people who professed faith in Jesus were often viewed as ignorant Bible thumpers or a cult. However, he always had a sense of God's existence—he was the one who led family prayers at mealtimes—but he said, "When there was a conflict between believing in God and doing what I wanted, I always sided with what I wanted to do."

As Kimberley and Henry continued to attend this new church, they began spending a lot of time in the Word with a patient associate pastor. In his mind, Henry pictured arriving in Heaven and being interviewed by Saint Peter (which he half-believed happened), and having Peter ask, "How do you think I can let you in if, during your time on earth, you read thousands of books but never read the Bible, the most important book of all time, the best-selling book in the world?"

Henry decided to read the Bible, but like he had done throughout high school, he read the "cliff notes"—only the New Testament. His first time through the New Testament actually turned him away from God because he thought Jesus had a God complex and because the exclusivity of faith did not seem compatible with an all-loving God. During his second read-through, however, Henry realized this could not be made up.

During this time, Kimberley and Henry had been continually debating which church was right—the liberal churches they'd grown up in or this new "born-again" church. One Sunday in 1998, Henry told Kimberley he thought this new church was right. She remarked calmly, "You know, I made that decision two weeks ago." Henry said, "So while our decision to come to faith happened somewhat independently of each other, our journey has been mutual ever since. (And we're also much better now at communicating life-changing decisions in real time.)"

BUSINESS PARTNERS AND VALUES

In 1999, a year before selling Chapel Hill Brokers, Henry started Bandwidth International, a company that sold the next big tradable commodity—bandwidth. Because he'd always wanted to travel with Kimberley, he based the company in London and spent the next two and a half years building the company there.

In 2000, God brought Henry a business partner. Henry cold-called the founder of Bandwidth.com, David Morken, simply to discuss purchasing David's website URL. But just the day before, David had been praying under his desk for two hours asking God to send him a business partner. Henry and David met in North Carolina, went biking, and by the end of the day they had established not only a business partnership, but also a friendship.

As Henry and David discussed what they wanted their company to look like, they knew it must have a set of values that drove their culture. One night at dinner, they decided on four values: faith, family, work, and fitness—in that order.

For examples of their values in action, all their employees are challenged to go home by 6 p.m. Henry said, "We're all too aware we have two hours a day to be a dad during the week. For us, it's the hours of six thirty to eight thirty p.m. We cherish that time with our families and we want our employees to have that as well." As for fitness, David and Henry exercise for an hour and a half during lunch, as do two-thirds of their employees. In fact, some of their partner retreats and senior management trips have revolved around fitness: they have ridden mountain stages during the Tour de France, gone surfing in Costa Rica, and have been heli-skiing several times.

> We're all too aware we have two hours a
> day to be a dad during the week.

Henry and David also founded Durham Cares, an organization that helps others care about their neighbors. It provides an overview of issues plaguing Durham, lists ways to get involved, has a volunteer match service, and generally raises the visibility of issues. It was created with hopes that other cities could reproduce it.

"We haven't always done [our Bandwidth values] well," Henry said, "but we've always endeavored to do it well. For example, it took us five years to feel comfortable praying with non-believing employees and ten years to hire a corporate chaplain. That was a mistake." And Henry can freely admit that mistake because it is part of their culture. An early Bandwidth motto was, "We suck less every day." Henry said, "While it was a little crude, it explains we make mistakes, but we learn from them and are better tomorrow. It also promotes an environment of forgiveness."

UNCERTAINTY

In the first year of Bandwidth's existence, they had twenty-five employees and $74,000 in revenue. So, as all good entrepreneurs do, they went up and down the West Coast meeting with investors. As Henry met with investors, he made it clear what drove him. He said, "We wouldn't necessarily mention it in the first presentation, but when it got to the second or third visit, particularly the site visit, we'd tell people about our values. It's not that we were trying to convert them—that's what God does—but we really needed them to understand why we did what we did." Overall, Henry met with forty investors, and while many expressed interest, none of them ultimately chose to invest.

In the midst of this financial uncertainty, Bandwidth received a contract for an OC3 circuit, which is a massive Internet pipeline that would lead to a large payday. One rule Bandwidth has is that they will not do business with the adult entertainment industry, even though it is the largest relative consumer of Internet access. The company buying the OC3 looked clean. There were lots of high fives as Bandwidth anticipated the deal. However, in provisioning the circuit, they discovered the corporation was merely a holding company for other companies in the adult entertainment business.

Henry said, "The big dilemma wasn't whether we would provision the circuit and get the payday—we knew our faith and our values would not allow that—but whether we would pay the sales rep a commission for the deal. We cancelled the deal with the company and determined the rep had done the requisite amount of diligence on the deal, so we paid his commission. It was the lowest cash point in our business. It was also the very point from which our company turned around. Over the next five years, from 2003 to 2007, we were the fourth fastest growing privately held company in the country. We achieved this growth—zero to eight-five million dollars (and it has since grown to more than two hundred million)—without getting institutional capital or making an acquisition."

At this point, Henry had only been a Christian for a few years, but when asked how he could make such a strong stand for his values, he said, "If you come to faith, particularly as I did—by trying to understand if Scripture is true or not—and you come to the realization that it is true, and you accept it all…that changes everything. In some ways, maybe it's easier for an adult convert. Everything changes. Who we work for, how we work…it's just different."

In 2009, Henry left Bandwidth to start Sovereign's Capital, an emerging markets venture funder that invests in Christian-led companies in the healthcare, IT, and consumer products and services fields. Of all the regions that are part of the 10/40 Window, Southeast Asia has become the fund's primary area of focus. Not only does Southeast Asia have a vibrant economy, but it also has great Christian businesses that are seeking to honor God in their work and be faithful witnesses in an otherwise Islamic culture.

THE WHY OF GIVING

Shortly after Henry and Kimberley came to faith, they began giving between 10 and 20 percent of all that they made. However, nothing radically changed until one day in 2009 when Daryl, one of Henry's friends, challenged him: "Henry, *why* do you give?"

Henry, **why** do you give?

Henry said something about God giving them a lot so they wanted to give back. "However, in the back of my mind, I was thinking Kimberley and I were probably giving twenty percent now—double tithing. There's probably a place in Heaven for the double-tithers. Maybe you get box seats to the Angels' games. And I was thinking that God would be happy with our giving because He needed our money to fund things that weren't being funded. Ultimately, it was bad theology."

That question brought Henry back to Scripture, to passages like 2 Corinthians 8:9 where it explains the difference between wealth and poverty. Henry said, "God took five loaves and two fish and fed five thousand. He doesn't need our money. He wants our hearts. Now we can give much more radically. We intend to give away half, and the lion's share of the rest is invested in Christian-led private companies in Asia."

Today, Henry is passionate about sending the message of biblical generosity worldwide through ministries like GenerosityMovement.org. He said, "Since God doesn't need our money, the aggregate amount of money doesn't matter. It's about heart transformation. So what does it look like to bring that message to the poorest of the poor in India?"

As he concluded, Henry said, "It really is true that it is more blessed to give than to receive—it's not just a Hallmark card saying. There's an incredible joy when you participate in the work of God. It's remarkably fulfilling because it fills up the hole that would otherwise contain idols that take the place of God."

YOUR STORY:

1. Henry and David led Bandwidth's corporate culture by ex-
    ample—they exercise regularly over lunch, are intention-
    al about spending time at home, and wouldn't do a large
    job that compromised their values. How are you influenc-
    ing the culture of your work or home? How can you lead by
    example?

2. A turning point in Henry's generosity journey was when
    a friend challenged him about why he gave. Up until that
    point, Henry had been feeling pretty good about himself
    because he'd been "double-tithing" and because God "need-
    ed" his money. What thoughts cross your mind as you think
    about your own giving? Why do you give?

3. Read 2 Corinthians 8. This was an influential chapter
    for Henry as he read how the apostle Paul challenged the
    Corinthians to "excel in this grace of giving" by telling them
    about the Macedonian churches whose "overflowing joy
    and…extreme poverty welled up in rich generosity." What
    do true wealth and poverty look like?

GENEROSITY

DAVE LINDSEY
DEFENDER Direct (Indianapolis, IN)

CHAPTER 6

SUPER SERVICE AND HOLY BUSINESS

For years, their dream only existed as a Post-it® note on Dave and Jessica Lindsey's mirror: "Build a business and build a family." Today, that dream is now the reality of DEFENDER Direct, a $450 million home security, heating, cooling, and plumbing company that has taken the Lindsey family on quite a spiritual and business journey. Dave and Jessica worked for several Fortune 500 companies after getting married, but always kept in mind their desire to start their own business. So in 1998 they moved home to Indiana to start a family and their own business.

INTENTIONAL COMPANY CULTURE

In the early days of the business, Dave focused on making payroll and ensuring all the bills were paid, and Jessica made sure they continued to tithe out of the company profits. They also felt led to give on a more frequent, quarterly basis instead of an annual one. "We tried to tithe real time as we were being blessed," Dave said. "We wanted a generous heart to be part of our work. Even in the early days when we were struggling, we didn't want to hold so tightly to every last penny. And we really feel like God has blessed that."

Another early factor that influenced the company's direction was Jim Rohn's book *The Art of Exceptional Living*. It stated that every company has a culture, so it's a good idea to create one on purpose. The idea excited Dave and he eventually founded his business on the following four passions:

1. **Self-Improvement**—commit to work harder on yourself than you do on your job.

2. **Systems Are the Solution**—create fully developed systems that produce predictable, repeatable, and scalable results.

3. **Developing Leaders**—once you have systematized learning, you can now share it with others and develop their leadership skills.

4. **Ever-Expanding Influence**—as we keep developing more leaders, our influence expands to more teams, families, companies, and other organizations.

Dave chose those four passions because he lives by the statement, "Businesses don't grow; people do." He has always believed that if he could grow his people, then the business would succeed. In fact, on every employee's first day they are told, "We want you to work harder on yourself than you do on your job." The idea is that if people work harder on themselves, they will grow, which ultimately leads to growth for the business.

GROWING ALONGSIDE EMPLOYEES

Another element of generosity is providing resources and opportunities for others' growth. As Dave and his family have enjoyed learning experiences, such as good business books, service opportunities, and training seminars, they have found ways to share those experiences with their employees.

For example, a friend invited the Lindseys to build a house for an underprivileged family in Mexico through Homes of Hope, a division of YWAM (Youth with a Mission). This experience radically changed how Dave and Jess saw generosity, their place in the world, and loving the poor. As soon as they returned, Dave planned the same trip to Mexico with his entire management team so they could have the same experience and translate it into the company culture.

DEFENDER Direct now sends approximately eight hundred people to Mexico every year. The company pays all the expenses for any employee (and family) who wants to go on the trip. In the last fifteen years, Homes of Hope has built over four thousand houses, two hundred of which were built in the last six years by DEFENDER Direct employees and their families.

Eventually, the Lindseys formalized the opportunities they wanted employees to have by creating a Monopoly-type board program, The DEFENDER Leadership Advantage. Employees are introduced to the program on their first day. The board contains activities like "Attend a Dave Ramsey class," "Build a house in Mexico," "Volunteer locally with Junior Achievement," "Read *Good to Great*," etc. The company pays for all the expenses, but it is the employee's responsibility to sign up for each opportunity. Each side of the board takes about a year to complete, although it does not have to be completed in order. As employees go around the board, they begin to learn and speak the same language as the company culture.

SIX MONTHS OF SWEET HARDSHIP

As the Lindseys became more involved with Homes of Hope, they also heard about YWAM's six-month Discipleship Training School (DTS). They had been givers for a number of years and served on several nonprofit boards, but this time the Lord said, "I want you to go to the other side of the table and learn what it's like to *be* the missionary."

Dave made arrangements for a top employee to become president, and then the Lindseys and their three children embarked on their six-month DTS journey. After three months of being discipled at YWAM's largest base in Kona, Hawaii, they moved to Takamatsu, Japan, right after the 2011 tsunami.

During the three months they lived in Japan, they worked with local churches, taught English, and evangelized while living in a one-bedroom Japanese apartment with three twenty-five-year-old YWAM guys. The five Lindseys shared the bedroom while the three young men slept in the living room. Together, the group of eight shared one bathroom and a tiny kitchenette.

Dave said, "It was one of the hardest things we ever did, but it was also one of the best things. It's interesting how sometimes suffering with the Lord is another kind of sweetness. At our home now, we all have our time apart. If the kids are bothering me, I can go read in my office. But in Japan, we were just stripped of all our abilities to escape—and that made us close. However, it didn't make us close because we were together—that kind of environment can make you really dislike people. It forced us to work through it, and, in the end, we found the only thing that could get us through our days was just praying together and asking the Holy Spirit to comfort us. And for the kids to see us praying that way, and to see our vulnerabilities—that was really powerful."

SUPER SERVING

When Dave returned to DEFENDER, the company had continued to thrive. One of the results of Dave's time away was another idea for company service and generosity—the Super Service Challenge (SSC). DEFENDER employees already enjoyed a charity day program that allowed them four to five days off a year to volunteer at one of the variety of charities on the company's menu. Now through the SSC, Dave encouraged employees to enter this contest and coordinate volunteer days so they could take their co-workers and serve at any nonprofit of their choice.

The power is that employees decided where to serve, not the company. Then, while the group was serving, they were asked to create a two-minute picture slideshow or video to capture the impact of the day. Finally, they answered three questions: 1) What did you accomplish? 2) What is your ongoing plan for a relationship with this nonprofit? 3) What would this nonprofit do if they were given $5,000 or $10,000? An independent group of judges then reviewed the videos and questions, and the top 20 percent of teams won $5,000 or $10,000 for the charity they served.

> We went from being a giving company
> to a company of givers.

Dave said, "We went from being a giving company to a company of givers. It is really fun to work at a company full of givers. The Challenge even changed the conversations around the water cooler—now people stand around and talk about what neat things other teams have done. It's creating what every company wants: more loyalty, more teamwork, and more motivation. We could offer more seminars and better comp plans in an attempt to motivate people, but when you send people out and let them serve, it really bonds them. Then they work better together on the next sale or installation because of the bond they are developing."

REACHING OTHER COMPANIES

Other companies began asking about the Super Service Challenge, so in 2013, DEFENDER expanded the contest nationwide, allowing anyone to sign up their workplace to compete for more than $1 million in prize money for charities. Dave also founded Companies with a Mission (www .cwam.com) to sponsor the Challenge and to encourage other businesses and their employees to live generously.

Dave also expanded the DEFENDER Leadership Advantage program to include trueU, which allows companies to sign up for the four-year leadership experience. Dave's dream is that three million people world-wide will complete trueU.

It takes time to develop these programs, but Dave is excited for the future. He said, "If you ask any anthropologist or scholar, they will tell you every society has seven spheres of life: government, education, family, communications/media, religion, business, and arts/entertainment. Every society always has a form of business and that is the sphere where I believe we are called. There is a greater purpose for our business than simply making money. Business in itself is actually holy—God created business. Just like there's a holy way to run a church, there's a holy way to run a business. And if you're running your business in a holy way, it will be blessed and produce fruit."

> Just like there's a holy way to run a church,
> there's a holy way to run a business.

THE M&M STORY

Dave summarizes his thoughts on generosity in a parable he tells his children: "Imagine a little kid with ten M&Ms sitting in a classroom during snack time. Some of the other kids have a lot of candy, but other kids have none. Would we encourage the kid with ten pieces to share one M&M (ten percent) with those who have none? Yes. It's not just because some of the other kids don't have M&Ms, but also because we want that kid to live with his hands open. We know a generous kid will have a more joyful life and better relationships if he doesn't squeeze his M&Ms and hide in a corner to eat them one at a time.

"Also, if that kid chooses to give, yes, another kid who doesn't have candy will get some, but the other thing is yet a third kid might have a few Snickers bars and say, 'Hey, I'll give you one of my Snickers if you give me some M&Ms. Thanks for sharing.'

"That is why we encourage tithing. It's not a guilt trap because someone needs M&Ms, but, instead, when you live with your hands open instead of closed, you'll be amazed at what ends up in your hands."

Your Story:

1. Every business has a culture: how people talk, what the atmosphere is like, what people value, etc. How would you describe the culture of your workplace or even your home? How might you create positive change by introducing generosity to that arena?

2. The Lindseys enjoy sharing helpful learning experiences with others. These things include financial seminars, building houses in Mexico, volunteering locally, etc. What experiences have been influential in your personal growth? What experiences could you repeat or share with your co-workers, friends, or family?

3. Dave said, "Business in itself is actually holy—God created business. Just like there's a holy way to run a church, there's a holy way to run a business." Many businessmen and church leaders alike often struggle with this concept either in practice or theory. What do you think about this statement? How can you see, encourage, or practice holy business?

4. In Dave's M&M story, he discusses tithing not as a guilt trap, but as a way of choosing to live with your hands open. Spend some time praying about where you might be holding on with closed fists. What is a practical step you can take to release control?

PURPOSEFUL GENEROSITY

Then the King will say to those on His right, "Come, you who are blessed by my Father, inherit the kingdom prepared for you from the foundation of the world. For I was hungry and you gave Me food, I was thirsty and you gave Me drink, I was a stranger and you welcomed Me, I was naked and you clothed Me, I was sick and you visited Me, I was in prison and you came to Me....Truly, I say to you, as you did it to one of the least of these my brothers, you did it to Me."

—MATTHEW 25:34-36, 40

GENEROSITY

RICK WARREN
Saddleback Church (Lake Forest, CA)

CHAPTER 7

A THOUSAND
LITTLE GIFTS

Imagine that you've worked hard for twenty-two years, built your business from the ground up, grown to twenty thousand employees, and finally the payday comes—the chance to cash out and live in luxury. What would you do?

While it wasn't a business, Rick Warren, Senior Pastor of Saddleback Church, was confronted with a similar choice—the chance to earn a small fortune and live the easy life or carry on just as before. Ultimately, the influence of his family, the valley of depression, and a thousand little gifts along the way made the path he took possible.

FAMILY INFLUENCES

Rick was the second child of Jimmy and Dot Warren. His father was a Baptist pastor and his mother was a school librarian. They were poor, but their meager means didn't entail a meager lifestyle. "My dad planted a garden that was an acre in size, which was far more than we could ever eat," Rick said. "But he wanted to give away the extra vegetables to provide for families in need."

His mother was a model of generosity as well. "When I woke up, I never knew who was going to be at the breakfast table because my parents were always taking in people, having guests or people who just needed help." One year, Rick's father added it up—Rick's mother had given away over one thousand additional meals in a single year!

Not only did Rick's parents model generosity, but they also taught him four big things not to do with money: "Don't waste it, don't love it, don't trust in it for security, and don't expect it to satisfy you." Those lessons would become important later in Rick's story.

> Don't waste it, don't love it, don't trust in it for security, and don't expect it to satisfy you.

THE CALL AND RELEASE OF A PASTOR

After graduating from high school, Rick attended California Baptist University. In November 1973, he and a friend skipped classes and drove three hundred fifty miles to hear W.A. Criswell preach. Rick stood in line to shake Criswell's hand, and Criswell told Rick he felt led to lay his hands on him and pray for him. This was a memorable moment in Rick's early ministry.

During seminary, Rick had a vision for building a church for people who didn't go to church. He believed that one day God would give him a church with twenty thousand people in attendance on a hundred-acre property. In April 1980, they led the first service of Saddleback Church at Laguna Hills High School with two hundred people in attendance.

After Saddleback Church began, it continued to grow quickly. They had to change locations often just to accommodate the church's growth. The crazy success of the church produced unintended consequences for Rick—depression. After the Christmas service in 1980, Rick fled to the Arizona desert where he found himself doubting his ability to lead a large congregation and questioning their success. In the desert, God made it clear to Rick that this ministry effort was not about Rick, but about the work God desired to do. "God reminded me that it was His church and He would take the responsibility for growing it. I had to let go of the reins and trust God."

A Thousand Gifts

As the church grew, so did Rick's opportunity for income. Nonetheless, he and Kay had made the decision to raise their giving each year of their marriage. Some years were lean, but still each year they increased their giving. And for thirty-eight years, they've kept that commitment.

Even in college, Rick found God was giving him opportunities to trust Him. At the end of one school year, he owed $500 in tuition that had to be paid by the end of the month in order to return to school the next year. He also owed a friend $10 for gas money. Rick had no money except for $50 in a savings account.

He reasoned that the $50 wasn't enough to pay his bills, so he closed out the account and, after praying, gave the money to the American Bible Society. He sent the $50 with a note saying, "Whoever gets this note, while you're processing this gift, would you mind praying for this poor college student who has some bills to pay? I'm trusting God to meet my needs as I think about the needs of other people."

About ten days later, Rick was invited to speak at a weekend revival at a church in Los Angeles. At the end of the revival, to his surprise, the pastor of the church took up an offering for him. That night Rick walked out with a check in the amount of $565, which meant he could pay his $500 tuition, the $10 loan, and $55 in tithes!

Along the way, Rick and Kay, in addition to their regular systematic giving, have also practiced strategic giving and spontaneous giving. "Kay has a policy that if she sees anybody on the corner she will always stop and give them something. Sometimes it's money and other times it's gift cards to grocery stores. While some people might say don't do that because they'll spend it on drugs or beer, you know what? That's their problem. If you have the opportunity, do it.

"I believe that spontaneous giving is just good for your heart—if you only do strategic giving, then you are trying to control everything. And that is a heart issue that needs to be exposed."

> I believe that spontaneous giving is
> just good for your heart.

One of Rick's favorite generosity stories happened over a four-year time span. While at some meetings in eastern Los Angeles, he and a friend went to a taco joint at midnight for a snack. A homeless man was outside the restaurant, so Rick bought him some burritos and something to drink.

Four years later and sixty miles away in Pasadena, Rick was waiting for his wife and son to finish an appointment. He bought lunch and sat outside on some church steps to eat. Two homeless men joined him, so he offered to split his lunch with the men. After a fun lunch of eating and telling stories, one of the men said, "I know who you are. You're Pastor Rick." When Rick asked him how the man knew him, the man replied, "Four years ago, on the other side of town, you bought me dinner at midnight."

Rick said, "That the guy would remember that, and that God gave me the opportunity to help him again, was just a neat confirmation that I was doing the right thing."

THE CHOICE

By 1995, just fifteen years after its inception, Saddleback Church had grown to ten thousand weekly attendees. In 1995, Rick also published *The Purpose Driven Church,* and followed that in 2002 with

The Purpose Driven Life: What on Earth Am I Here For? It hit number one on four major best-seller lists, including *The New York Times, The Wall Street Journal, USA Today,* and *Publishers Weekly. Time* magazine named him one of the "15 Leaders Who Mattered Most in 2004," and in 2005 he was named one of the "100 Most Influential People in the World."

Today, *The Purpose Driven Life* has sold more than 32 million copies worldwide and is the most-translated book in the world next to the Bible. A best-selling book like that means millions of dollars.

So what do you do with those millions? The same thing you've been doing for thirty-eight years—you give them away. "Honestly, the money scared me," Rick said. "But I knew I wasn't going to spend it on myself. When you write a book and the first sentence of the book is 'It's not about you,' then you know the money is not for you. I was taught that God was using money to test me. My use of money shows what I love the most."

Rick and Kay made the decision to give away 90 percent of the proceeds and to live on 10 percent. Their decision was simply consistent with the way they'd been living. Rick noted, "Luke 16:11-12 says whoever can be trusted with very little, can also be trusted with much. But whoever is dishonest with very little, will be dishonest with much. If you have not been trustworthy with handling worldly wealth, who will trust you with the true riches?"

In commenting on this passage Rick said, "I believe there's a direct connection between maturity and money, between spiritual power and possessions, between how much God is able to bless you and how good a money manager I am. And if God cannot trust you with material blessing, He's not going to give you spiritual power. And I'm far more interested in the power and the anointing and the blessing of God."

If God cannot trust you with material blessing,

He's not going to give you spiritual power.

THE IMPACT

What are the results? Rick still drives a fourteen-year-old Ford, wears a watch from Wal-Mart, and still lives in the same home they bought years ago. "I'm not into a lot of bling. I'm happy if I've got a good pair of jeans and a t-shirt. I think part of it has to do with your own self-esteem and security in Christ. If you know *who* you are because you know *whose* you are, then you don't need status symbols and name brands on your luggage to prop you up. So in other words, I don't have to buy a fancy suit to feel like I'm a good preacher."

On the other hand, their giving has touched many. Rick has given heavily to equip leaders by training pastors around the world, including those in little villages no one would know. Kay has led the charge in supporting the work of orphans and HIV and AIDS work around the world. They've launched a well-publicized and received Global PEACE plan to plant churches, equip servant leaders, assist the poor, care for the sick, and educate the next generation.

"Sometimes people ask me, 'Why do you think God chose you to be the author of the best-selling hardback book in American history?' I say, 'Well because He knew what I'd do with the money. He knew He could trust me.'" In answering those who say they would give it all away if they also had a lot of money, Rick said, "No you wouldn't because you're not giving it when you are poor."

Indeed, last year Rick and Kay raised their giving to 91 percent and lived off of just 9 percent. "And I have no intention of stopping there," Rick said. "I've played this game with God for thirty-eight years where God says, 'You give to Me, and I'll give to you, and let's see who wins.'"

YOUR STORY:

1. Rick Warren began to understand generosity because it was first modeled by his parents through things like having a large garden so his mother could offer meals to others. What heart attitude does your giving reflect? Is it an attitude you want to pass on to your children?

2. Rick said that to learn to be generous, we must first find our security in Christ rather than in status symbols like possessions or the logos on our luggage or clothing. What status symbols do you have in your life? Consider what their purpose is—do you use them to enjoy God and serve others, or do they serve as props for your identity and security?

3. Many people say they would give a lot of money if they suddenly became wealthy. However, Rick said if you're not already giving when you have little, that's not going to change when you have much. What steps do you need to take to be faithful with the time, talents, relationships, money, and possessions you now have?

4. Many people talk about the prayer of Jabez (*Lord, bless me and enlarge my territory*), but Rick thinks we should also learn the prayer of Agur in Proverbs 30, which essentially says, "Lord, don't let me become too poor or too rich, but just give me what I need. If I have too much, I might forget about You, but if I'm too poor, I might steal and disgrace Your name." How might this prayer be helpful for you as you balance how much is enough?

DAVID HAZELL
My Father's World (Rolla, MO)

CHAPTER 8

CHOOSING DIFFICULT DREAMS

It was very difficult to be a missionary behind the Iron Curtain in the 1980s, but difficult is what David Hazell wanted. And he intended to get there, even if it meant he had to buy a Trans-Siberian railroad ticket and throw his passport out the window. After David got married (which he said must have been God's plan to calm him down), he discarded some of his crazier ideas, but never lost his passion for creatively breaking barriers for the Kingdom of God.

Raised in a traditional Catholic family, David's journey toward Christ took a huge leap forward on a bike trip across Iowa when he was eighteen. Partway through the trip, he became ill. Not knowing where else to get help, he searched for a Christian bookstore and said, "I hear Christians are kind people…." The bookstore connected him with a Christian family who cared for him for six weeks while he recovered. While in their community, David was invited to a Christian rock concert where he committed his life to Christ.

PREPARING FOR DIFFICULT DREAMS

Shortly after he became a Christian, David began asking God for purpose. He dreamed about going somewhere difficult, somewhere no one had ever been before. He said, "I don't know why doing something hard was important to me, but I think God gave me a heart of adventure and He intends to use what He's given you."

> God gave me a heart of adventure and He intends to use what He's given you.

A few years later, David married Marie, a woman who shared his passion for God's Kingdom. At that time, she decided that a $5,000 reserve was more than enough to sustain a young family and everything else could be given away.

When David shared with Marie his dream for reaching Siberia, Mongolia, and Tibet, she thought that area was far too large for one family to reach. Over time, they narrowed their focus as God placed on their hearts the Evenki, a nomadic reindeer-herding tribe and unreached people group in Siberia, Mongolia, and Northern China.

It was a long road to the mission field. At one point, they were headed to China, but doors closed after the Tiananmen Square Massacre occurred. For thirteen years, David and Marie faithfully prayed for the Evenki while Marie taught schoolchildren in California and David worked on obtaining a master's degree in linguistics and taught ESL (English as a Second Language).

For them, waiting meant preparing. "When the Iron Curtain fell and other people were just beginning to get ready, we were already prepared to go," David said. "We began a family and lived in a remote cabin without running water. We had learned to garden and to hunt. We were out of debt. We were preparing for missions from the day we got married."

WANTED: SOMEONE TO LEARN RUSSIAN AND TRAVEL

In 1991, David and a church friend took an exploratory trip to Siberia and Mongolia. They discovered the Institute for Bible Translation in Moscow was working with the Evenki and needed someone who was willing to learn Russian and travel. The following year, David, Marie, and their five children (all under the age of nine) moved from Southern California to the Siberian taiga in the middle of winter where the temperature was thirty degrees below zero.

While they lived in Siberia for four years, David not only served on a Bible translation team but also coordinated Bible translation projects. Eventually, in order to manage projects more effectively, he and his family (now six children) moved to Moscow where he worked his way up to guiding twenty-seven projects. Then he moved on to the printing department where he turned the one-man department into an eight-person production team. David said, "I'm not really a details, on-the-ground person. I break through the barrier, and then I move on to break the next one, and the next one. God has taught me to replace myself and move on."

> I'm not really a details, on-the-ground person. I break through the barrier, and then I move on to break the next one.

LUKE'S THOUSAND-DOLLAR GOSPEL

One day in the printing department in Moscow, David discovered a project for the Bezhta, an unreached people group without a written language in the North Caucasus region of Russia. A linguist had already created an alphabet and translated the Gospel of Luke into Bezhta, but the book had been held off press for three years. David wanted to know why the project wasn't first in line, only to discover there were no sponsors. He asked how much it would cost to print a thousand copies of Luke and the answer almost made him cry: just $1,200 would bring the Gospel to these people for the first time.

David and Marie quickly found sponsors for the Gospel. Immediately after the books were printed and shipped, the Institute for Bible Translation began receiving telegraphs saying, "Thank you for putting our language into writing. Thank you for giving us God's Word." In fact, the region's Islamic government even mandated that whoever worked for the government and spoke Bezhta needed to read the Gospel of Luke as part of their work each day.

About this time, Marie was reminded of David's original dream to reach Siberia, Mongolia, and Tibet—an area she had thought was too large for one family to reach. "Look, honey," David said. "Today we're working with sixty-seven languages influencing forty Muslim groups, and reaching people throughout Russia, Mongolia, and China."

A BUSINESS BEGINS

After the Hazells realized it had only taken $1,200 to print the Bezhta Gospel of Luke, they wanted to start a business. If they could make a business succeed, they could give 50 percent of their income to fund Bible translation.

David's idea for a business was a kindergarten curriculum Marie had written before they moved overseas. He had circulated some manuscripts at a homeschool conference in the mid-90s. Soon after, an influential homeschool advocate, Cathy Duffy, contacted them and said it was one of the best kindergartens she had ever seen. She wanted to know if she could publish information about it in her next homeschool curriculum guide.

Although their curriculum was not yet in print, the Hazells agreed: "We believed by the time Cathy printed her homeschool guide, we could publish our curriculum." Miraculously, even though the Hazells remained in Russia, God provided a missionary printer and his wife who returned to the U.S. and published *My Father's World—Kindergarten*.

After the first year, they received many letters requesting a first grade curriculum. "Even though we don't have first grade," David said, "we have customers. We say yes. We developed pilot programs where consumers received lesson plans every six weeks as Marie finished writing the curriculum. We were amazed. People signed up to buy!"

The business grew too big for the Hazells to manage through friends and family while they stayed in Russia, so in 2000 they returned to the United States. Marie would teach school and David would turn the curriculum into a family business.

GOING ALL IN

But after just one year, Marie realized she couldn't teach school and write new curriculum at the same time. If she quit her job, however, they had just enough reserve funds to live for a year. "As is our habit," David said, "we faced each other and asked, 'Are you willing to start all over again if everything goes wrong and we are left with nothing?'"

Are you willing to start all over again if everything goes wrong and we are left with nothing?

They agreed and Marie quit her job. "We lived on the equity in our house," David said. "We went all in with everything we had. We prayed we would just sell one curriculum every day to support ourselves."

God provided and they ended the year with the same amount of money they began with. Did they want to do it again? Yes! So they pushed it all to the center of the table and went all in again. And they went all in each year until 2009, when the business was finally large enough to fund itself.

Initially, each year the business, My Father's World, doubled. In 2002, they hired their first full-time employee. The next year, they moved to Rolla, Missouri, to be closer to homeschool conferences and where the cost of living was lower. That year, their business grossed $230,000. In 2007, and again in 2010, they doubled their staff. In the meantime, they continued selling the next year's curriculum even before it was written, piloting programs in six-week increments. It worked. God blessed their efforts.

GENEROSITY GOALS

The entire time the Hazells were giving 50 percent of their income. "I don't think we had a passion to give large sums of money until 1998," David said. "Until that point, we just gave everything we had life-wise. There isn't much money to be given when you are living on missionary support."

When David and Marie left the mission field in 2000, they made a bold commitment to each other to raise a half million dollars annually for Bible translation within ten years. They chose that number because the Institute for Bible Translation was about a half million dollars short for annual expenses. "We haven't quite made that goal yet," David said, "but we keep trying. Our plan was to come back to the U.S., start a business, and raise the entire deficit of the Institute for Bible Translation in Moscow. Each year with God's help we get closer. We dream someday of giving more than fifty percent of our income."

BIG DREAMS FOR THE FUTURE

Today, David also runs God's Word for the Nations, a nonprofit founded in 2002. Their first commitment remains to give generously to Bible translation. However, going forward, the Hazells have bigger dreams to prepare leaders and missionaries to work for God's Kingdom. There are five key problems today's missionaries face, and the Hazells seek potential solutions to each of these shortcomings. The goal is to:

1. Train missionaries to resolve interpersonal conflict—this is the biggest reason people leave the field.

2. Prepare families for the hardship of raising a family in another culture, including recognizing and giving up a life of entitlement.

3. Provide missionaries extensive cross-cultural job training before they leave for the field.

4. Train missionaries in marketable life skills (carpentry, ESL, etc.) so they can provide for themselves should anything happen to their funding.

5. Counteract the idea that missionaries must fund raise. By creating businesses that provide funds for missionaries on the field as well as jobs for them when they return for furlough, they can focus on rejuvenating rather than raising funds.

To these ends, the Hazells are investing in properties that could become nonprofit training centers in the future. For example, they currently own a retreat center, a print shop, and a woodworking shop. They hope that someday missionaries on furlough could work in these businesses to earn money for themselves and others on the field while learning marketable skills like carpentry, accounting, and business. The woodworking shop could provide furnishings for the retreat center (cedar benches, signs, chairs, etc.) as well as selling the same items to generate funds for worldwide ministry.

David also hopes to increase their local mission field by starting an English as a second language school to draw international students to Rolla, Missouri. Tuition fees would support the ministry and, in turn, the school's staff (missionaries-in-training) would learn to sensitively present the claims of the Gospel to a cross-cultural community.

When asked where his ideas come from, David said, "God has given us a mind. He seems to speak to us through ideas, hunches, and impressions. As we speak these thoughts aloud, they begin to take form. It's both amazing and fun."

Your Story:

1. When David and Marie married, they decided that a $5,000 emergency fund was enough for their family at the time. While this number will be different for everyone and may change at different life stages, what is that current number for your family?

2. David's big dream is ultimately to help others spread the Word of God so those who have not heard can receive it. However, what this looks like has drastically changed over the years: prayer warrior for the Evenki for thirteen years, missionary in Siberia, Bible project coordinator in Moscow, curriculum business owner, and founder of a nonprofit. What is your big dream? How have you seen it take various forms over your lifetime?

3. It was a catalytic moment in David's life when he realized it only took $1,200 to print the Gospel of Luke for an un-reached people group. Research ministries like God's Word for the Nations, the Institute for Bible Translation, Faith Comes by Hearing, One Verse, Wycliffe Bible Translators, etc. Could God be prompting you to join the Hazells in giving to Bible translation?

4. Today, David is hoping to start a new nonprofit to address the needs of missionaries based on what he observed on the field. What needs around you have you seen over your lifetime? How might your experience or expertise be able to address those needs to advance the Kingdom?

JIM BLANKEMEYER
MetoKote Corporation (Lima, OH)

CHAPTER 9

THE SHAPE OF MY LIFE AND GOD'S MISSION

No story is perfect. There are always bumps and bruises along the way, but the key is to learn the lessons that come from those knocks. Jim Blankemeyer came from modest means. His father was a farmer and Jim himself never went to college. He calls himself an engineer type—he enjoys working with his hands and making discerning, informed decisions. After starting a successful metal coating business, Jim came to know Christ. From there, he has continued to learn to respond to the activity God puts in front of him.

EARLY FAMILY LESSONS

Jim grew up seeing his parents model generosity in very practical ways. Not only was Jim's father a farmer, but he was also an excellent mechanic who could overhaul tractors, cars, and just about anything that had an engine or gears. Because these were the waning years of the Great Depression (Jim was born in 1935), Jim's father regularly helped his neighbors by repairing their cars for very little or even deferring payment for a year or more until the neighbor could repay him.

Jim's mother provided meals and clothing to hobos and those who walked the railroads. Both of Jim's parents were willing to share the little they had with others who were in even more difficult situations. Jim and his siblings were also taught to save their pennies so they could give to the church and missions.

BUSINESS DECISIONS AND DIRECTION

After a brief stint in the National Guard, Jim worked at a metallurgical lab where he discovered the need for a metal coating to protect specialized grinding and cutting machines from corrosive acids and electrical discharge. At the time, virtually no other businesses offered these coating services.

In the summer of 1969, Jim decided to start his own metal coating business. With the skills acquired from his mechanic-welder father and carpenter uncle, and with his wife's wholehearted support, Jim was confident the business could succeed. He rented a garage near Lima, Ohio, for $50 a month and purchased some machinery from an industrial junkyard. He cut the equipment apart, rewired the electrical panels, reassembled the oven and conveyor system to suit his needs, and MetoKote Corporation was in business.

Within five years, the business was already winning contracts with major corporations like GM and Ford. However, the business growth took a heavy toll in time away from his family and he knew something needed to change. Jim and his wife, Carolyn, started attending a Bible study that eventually moved into their home. Several months later, they committed their lives to Christ.

Gradually, Jim began to refocus his priorities. Instead of striving for success for the sake of success, he began asking God to glorify Himself through the resources He had placed in Jim's life. Oddly enough, when Jim placed the company in God's hands, the business began experiencing rapid growth, and within the next twenty years his company had built over forty coating/painting/industrial finishing plants in ten countries. Today, they have over three thousand employees worldwide.

With this newfound commitment to the Lord, Jim began asking what God truly wanted from him. "Okay, Lord," he said, "do You really want me in business or am I to do something else?" At that point of his life, with six children at the time, the idea of being a missionary or pastor was pretty much out of the question. As Jim continued to read the Bible, however, 1 Corinthians 7:24 stood out to him: "So, brothers, in whatever condition each was called, there let him remain with God." For Jim, it confirmed that he should stay in business—that was where he was gifted and that's what he was supposed to do.

> "So, brothers, in whatever condition each was called, there let him remain with God." —1 CORINTHIANS 7:24

DISCERNING GOD'S CALL

As Jim looks back on those early years of commitment to the Lord, he calls himself a naïve giver. Often, he would give to almost anyone who asked and claimed Christian values or beliefs. But after a while, he realized this was not very good discernment or stewardship. Not only was he failing to discern the real need of the request, but he was also dissipating his attention, time, and energy. Instead, he began asking, "Okay, Lord, what have You called me to do? How have You shaped my life to fit Your mission?"

Jim knew he should take care of his family, those around him, the poor and the needy, and so forth. But even that was a struggle because he knew that no matter how many resources he gave, there would still be the poor and needy. There had to be godly discernment.

As Jim pondered this, he thought about how his company was able to prosper—one of the main ingredients was training employees. As the company built new plants, they would bring in their new employees—everyone from repairmen to plant managers—and train them for an extended period of time. He knew these new employees needed certain skill sets to work with his specialized machinery and to be really productive for the company.

As Jim traveled frequently for work and ministry, he saw the disparity between how his company trained employees and how the church often worked, especially in underdeveloped areas of the world. The dilemma in his mind became, "There is a huge emphasis on spiritual conversion and evangelism, but very little on follow-up, training, and discipleship. We have a lot of church leaders in these underdeveloped parts of the world with little real training. Many times, it's because they lack opportunity. These leaders needed access to well-rounded spiritual training, mentorship, and leadership skills."

As Jim continued to see this trend worldwide, he recognized his call: "Okay, Lord. This is an area I've sensed a great need and I believe You've called me to it, so that's what I'm going to focus on. You've gifted us in this area of training, and if we're doing it for our earthly business, we ought to do it for the church also." So Jim began supporting and encouraging seminaries, Bible schools, and training institutions.

> You've gifted us in this area of training, and
> if we're doing it for our earthly business,
> we ought to do it for the church also.

EXPERIENCING GIVING WITH CHILDREN

At home, as Jim's (now) nine children grew older, it became clear he would either have to sell or transition his company in some way. Because the company was rapidly gaining in value, and, more importantly, in the best interest of his family, employees, and customers, Jim wanted to prepare his children for the eventual sale of the company. He also wanted his children to experience the same things he and his wife had as they gave to Christian training and leadership development.

In 1988, as Jim's older children were into their college and early career years, Jim and Carolyn started a private family foundation with a focus on church leadership development. Their desire was to encourage, educate, and ignite a passion in their children for generosity as God would lead them.

There are a variety of ways Jim and his wife have encouraged their children to be generous. First, they began to be more open about their finances and the potential value of the company. Up until that point, their children did not really know how well the company was doing. They began discussing their financial situation along with how, why, and how much they gave to specific organizations.

Secondly, they took family trips to see the places they supported. For example, they visited a seminary in Columbia to let their children not only experience the culture, but also to see how much the seminary students sacrificed to get a biblical education.

In addition to their own children, they also committed to taking their grandchildren on trips to mission sites once they were young teenagers. These "grandkid trips," as they are called, are primarily to seminaries and Bible schools, but they also include visits to prisons and garbage dumps to show their grandkids how much of the world lives.

As far as the family foundation goes, the entire family meets as a foundation once a year. They bring in consultants from most of the continents to give an update on their area of the world, not just in terms of ministry but also regarding the geo-political, economic, and religious climates.

These meetings are structured as a typical business meeting with agendas and reports. The family makes recommendations and decisions on the various grant proposals the foundation has received. All of the children are encouraged to be part of the process and to get involved.

The foundation has a formal mission and vision statement and giving guidelines. Within their focus of church leadership development, they emphasize what they call "compassionate giving guidelines." Jim said, "We don't believe a leader is an effective leader unless he has a Christlike heart, and Christ had a heart of compassion. So we try to design a giving plan that encourages leaders to develop and experience that compassionate heart of Christ."

The Blankemeyers choose to be very intentional about their giving because they believe God has called them to focus on leadership development. But they also recognize the importance of keeping an open heart as spontaneous generosity opportunities arise.

RELATIONAL GIVING

The Blankemeyers also believe in the importance of having personal relationships within the ministries they support. Jim said, "I've heard it said a person can only maintain a serious, engaging relationship with a few people, ten at most, and a much less personal relationship with perhaps ten to twenty people. If we spread ourselves too thin, we not only dissipate our funds, but also our time and energy. Ministry leaders and individuals need to have relationships and we have a responsibility to each other in terms of developing and maintaining those relationships."

On a more practical level, these relationships must be built on an understanding of the individual's family, their wishes, needs, and concerns. Jim said, "I've found that unless we open ourselves to one another, the relationship will always be very superficial and shallow. We all have the same needs, concerns, and problems, and we need to support one another in those areas. We have had situations where an individual in ministry has shared concerns with us that they wouldn't normally tell others."

RETIREMENT PLANNING

The Blankemeyers' giving primarily comes from their family foundation that was established with profits from the business. When Jim turned sixty-five, he sold a major portion of the company. These funds, along with the remaining ownership of the company that was donated later, provide the base for the foundation's operations.

During Jim's career, his family never had an extravagant lifestyle. He and Carolyn never focused on amassing a large savings or retirement account. Instead, they wanted to be wise stewards and use their God-given resources as He directed. Jim said, "God has blessed us with many resources on this earth. However, my security is not in a large retirement plan or in a big bank account. We live very well and my family is provided for, so I am content."

He continued, "We have a grandchildren's college education fund. We believe it is important for our children and grandchildren to discern their own giftedness and to work for at least part of their education. If they choose not to use their college fund for formal education, they can withdraw limited amounts at certain ages. Additionally, we have a trust fund for our children and have communicated what they will be receiving so that they can plan for their own current and future stewardship responsibilities. God has blessed me abundantly. I have provided for my wife, my children, and grandchildren, so what more do I need?"

YOUR STORY:

1. Many decisions in Jim's life have been marked by prayers of, "Okay, Lord, what next?" or "What do You want me to do in this situation?" What prayers do you pray as you are deciding the next step to take?

2. Jim focuses his giving on Christian leadership development, something that reflects his personality (making wise decisions) and his passion at work (training people so they can succeed in their jobs). What is your personality and passion? How might God be using these to shape your giving habits?

3. Jim and his wife made a commitment to teach their children generosity and allow them to experience it through several avenues: talking openly about their finances and giving habits, establishing a family foundation, and taking trips to the ministries they support. How might you inspire a passion for generosity in your children or those around you?

UNCOMFORTABLE GENEROSITY

Do nothing from selfish ambition or conceit, but in humility count others more significant than yourselves. Let each of you look not only to his own interests, but also to the interests of others.

—Philippians 2:3-4

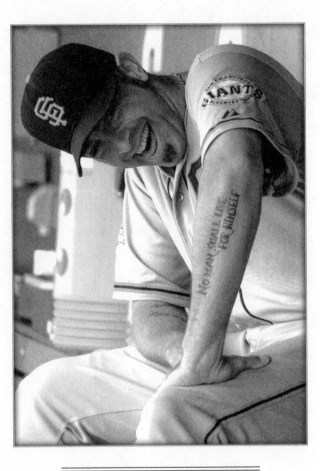

JEREMY AFFELDT
San Francisco Giants
(San Francisco, CA)

CHAPTER 10

REDISCOVERING THE LOVE OF THE GAME

How many students get drafted to play baseball right out of high school? This was left-handed pitcher Jeremy Affeldt's reality. However, after several years in the Major Leagues, he hated his dream; he wasn't sure he even wanted to play anymore. He was ready to leave the game behind unless God would give him a reason to stay.

SEARCHING FOR THE GOD WHO PROVIDES

Jeremy was born to a career military father, so he spent much of his childhood bouncing from location to location. As Jeremy rebelled against the frequent moves, he became known as a troublemaking, angry kid. In high school in Washington, Jeremy struggled with authority issues. He said, "All the pent-up rage exploded. I learned when I did something in anger, everybody would turn their attention toward me. I wanted to control the situation and I could. That's why I enjoyed sports."

Jeremy's excessive anger began limiting his playing time. That's when he began getting serious about his relationship with Christ. He actually began studying the Bible so he could keep playing basketball. As he read, he was stunned by the idea that Jesus died, in part, because He knew a rebellious kid named Jeremy would live two thousand years later and He loved that kid. That knowledge transformed Jeremy's life.

In 1997, right after high school, Jeremy was drafted into the Kansas City Royals farm team system. Those first years in the minor leagues were difficult financially, especially after Jeremy married and took on the responsibility of providing for his wife and high school sweetheart, Larisa. In the beginning, Jeremy was making $600 a month, but they still chose to give a portion of that. "It was not affordable. It wasn't easy or comfortable. But we were looking to Heaven and saying, 'If we believe You are our caregiver, if we believe You take care of us and You ask us to be cheerful givers, then we have to believe You will provide for us.' And God always did it."

This prayer was an expression of Jeremy's desire to make money so he could give it away. However, as a twenty-two-year-old, Jeremy was not sure if he would make it into the Major Leagues. But that same year, in 2002, his wife found a well-paying job and Jeremy was offered a Major League contract with the Royals. "Doors opened when they shouldn't have," Jeremy said. "I think those doors opening had a lot to do with my heart and desire to honor God and live generously."

THINGS GET BROKEN

Once in the Major Leagues, Jeremy found himself struggling again. He wasn't pitching well and kept getting injured. Also, during his four years with the Royals, they only had one winning season. As the Royals continued losing year after year, Jeremy experienced a familiar emotion: "I was angry because we lost all the time and I didn't know if I was going to be a starter or a reliever. I didn't know who I was in baseball anymore."

Exhausted, broken, tired of losing, and tired of not enjoying the game, Jeremy sat on the counter one day and cried as he told Larisa he wanted to quit. She responded, "That is not an option. I know it is tough, but it will be okay. Right now it's hard, but it's not going to be like this forever."

Jeremy continued to pray that God would either get him traded so he could get a fresh start or close the door on his baseball career. In 2006, he was traded to the Colorado Rockies—where he promptly had the worst season of his career. Jeremy was convinced he would not get another contract, but he prayed, "God, if You get me another contract, then I know You want me to keep playing. However, You'll have to show me what I'm playing baseball for. There isn't a lot of fulfillment if success is just being cheered by fifty thousand people you're paid to entertain."

At the end of 2006, Mike King, one of Jeremy's friends who runs YouthFront in Kansas City, told Jeremy about an idea he had for a hunger initiative, Something to Eat, that helps kids learn about and fight food poverty. When Jeremy heard the idea, he got excited: "This gives me a reason to keep playing baseball," he told Mike. "If I play, I can make money to financially support this thing."

> This gives me a reason to keep playing baseball.

Jeremy received another contract with the Rockies in 2007, and that year they went on to play in the World Series. And as Jeremy got more involved with the food initiative, he found his reason to keep playing: "I was finally pitching for a purpose and I enjoyed going to the park every day. That year, I went to the World Series for the first time, which was also the first time the Rockies had been."

A NEW PLATFORM

"I think God answered my heart's cry," Jeremy said. "I asked Him for direction, a reason to play, and a way to enjoy the game, and He did all that. Then, in 2009, I ended up winning the Setup Man of the Year Award after an amazing year in baseball. In 2010 and 2012, I won the

World Series with the San Francisco Giants. My platform had gotten big. I have a well-read blog and a book, *To Stir a Movement*. My speaking platform had gotten even bigger. Because of what's taken place in sports, I have an avenue to speak into so many areas."

Today, Jeremy believes that baseball is the platform God has given him to promote the Gospel and to give. Although he works very hard to perfect his skills, he knows that ultimately he hasn't received big contracts because of his talent, but because God has protected and blessed him. He said, "For me to honor Jesus, I need to think that this isn't my money or my career. This didn't have to happen. I've been protected from injury so I can play longer, which allows me to come into more money so I can bless others."

One of Jeremy's favorite stories happened while he was doing physical therapy. A young man approached him and said, "I wanted to let you know that your story really influenced me. I'm a runner and I'm about to go to South Africa with Athletes in Action to use my sport to influence people to know Jesus—and your story has been a big part of that."

As Jeremy has received more opportunities to grow his platform, he has continued to learn about poverty. He is now actively involved with several ministries that work with orphanages, fight sex trafficking, and provide water and food. These ministries include Not for Sale, Living Water International, Global Orphan Project, One World Fútbol, Something to Eat, and his own nonprofit, Generation Alive.

"I have a motto I live by: 'No man shall live for himself,'" Jeremy said. "It's basically 'Love your neighbor as yourself.' I believe we can end large areas of poverty. Will it completely end? I don't know. But I do know I'm called to Matthew 25 (that says feeding and clothing the least of these is like doing it for Jesus) and I find a lot of fulfillment in that as I give. Then when people ask me, 'Why are you doing this?' I can simply say, 'I love you.' And they'll say, 'You don't know me.' And I can say, 'But I have a love that doesn't come from needing to know you. I have the love of Jesus inside of me and I can return that to you.'"

LEARNING TO GIVE

When Jeremy was asked where he first learned to give, he said, "I used to give out of habit. I gave my ten percent because that's what I was supposed to do. But now it's more about being a cheerful giver. I'm in a sport that allows us to make lots of money, so I can make an impact financially. Not everyone is called to make a financial impact—there are other avenues for generosity—but I have that chance and that's what my wife and I want to do."

Jeremy was blessed to not only grow up with a family of givers, but to marry into one. His family modeled giving, so as a child Jeremy would save 10 percent of his allowance in an envelope so he could tithe. Especially after seeing poverty for several years while his father was stationed in Guam, Jeremy always had a sense of giving.

Then when Jeremy married, his father-in-law, a successful businessman, continued to model generosity. He encouraged Jeremy, "If you have the finances to do it, don't stop at ten percent—think outside the box. The New Testament no longer uses the word 'tithe' or mandates it; instead, it tells us to be cheerful givers."

Jeremy said, "I've learned you shouldn't just stop and say, 'I'm comfortable here; that's as far as I want to go with my giving.' Always think bigger. Always think your money was given to you for a purpose. You may not even call it a 'tithe,' but just support the Kingdom.

> Always think your money was given
> to you for a purpose.

"Some people think you should give everything to the church, but there are other ministries that are all pushing the Kingdom of God. I don't give to one place, but I ask the Spirit of God where He wants me to give. There are some areas I give to, but other areas where God says, 'I don't want you giving there because that's not where I'm calling you. I've got other people giving to them.' God sees the whole picture and knows what people need and where. So it's been a great time of asking the Spirit of God to show me where to give. I don't want to stay comfortable and miss an opportunity where the Gospel can be accomplished."

YOUR STORY:

1. When Jeremy and Larisa were making $600 a month starting out, they would pray, "If we believe You are our caregiver, if we believe You take care of us and You ask us to be cheerful givers, then we have to believe You will provide for us." If God asks us to give cheerfully, what does that say about His ability to also provide for us?

2. Some of Jeremy's favorite verses are Matthew 25:31-46. Prayerfully read this passage. What does it mean to live by Jeremy's motto: "No man shall live for himself"?

3. Ultimately, Jeremy knows he is still playing baseball because God has protected him and is using this platform, along with its finances, to advance the Kingdom of God. How is God using your current station in life for Kingdom work?

4. Jeremy's father-in-law encouraged him to think beyond the tithe because the New Testament no longer mandates it. Instead, the New Covenant tells us to be cheerful givers. How does your mindset (and/or giving) change when you begin thinking as a cheerful giver instead of as a tither?

VINCE ELLIOTT
Financial Advisor (Houston, TX)

CHAPTER 11

WEALTHY ENOUGH TO FIND PEACE

What does it mean to be wealthy and generous? Perhaps the more important question is, *What should we keep?* For most of his life, God has given Vince Elliott the opportunity—not always by choice—to wrestle with these questions. Corrie ten Boom said, "Hold everything in your hands lightly, otherwise it hurts when God pries your fingers open." This quote has been an inspiration to Vince in his journey.

LESSON ONE: WHAT WILL YOU KEEP?

Growing up in Highland Park, one of the wealthiest neighborhoods in Dallas, Texas, Vince saw considerable wealth around him. But his idea of wealth was challenged at Kanakuk Camps, a Christian camp in Missouri he attended every summer for twelve years either as a camper or counselor. Vince remembers the founder of Kanakuk and his hero, Joe White, teaching on the parable of the widow's mite. Joe told his group, "I am confident you are faithfully giving God the first fruits of your labor, the first ten percent. But what are you doing with the last ten percent?

Even if you've turned over ninety percent of your life to God, what are you still holding on to?"

Even if you've turned over 90 percent of your life to God, what are you still holding on to?

Vince had an early opportunity to test that equation. After moving from Highland Park to Houston, Vince entered a new high school. On his first day of school, he asked when the Young Life meetings were. Upon finding no one had heard of Young Life, he campaigned to get the first Young Life club started at Kincaid High School, earning himself the reputation of "Jesus freak" or "Bible thumper." With that title, he lost the opportunity to be known as the "cool guy."

However, when Vince went to college, he decided he was sick of being the good kid. "For a couple of years, I lived as worldly a life as my conscience would allow...the partying, the girls," Vince said. "I didn't lose my faith, and I knew what I was doing was wrong, but I just couldn't find my way back."

But one day, Patti McMullen walked into his life. He had never met a girl like her. Two weeks into dating, Vince knew he wanted to marry her. But he also knew he wasn't good enough for her. "I realized if I were her father or brother, I wouldn't let her date me, so I either needed to break up with her or change. I thought it was worth changing."

LESSONS ON GIVING AND LOSING

Vince moved back to Houston and started giving of his time as a Young Life leader. He also married Patti. "The Holy Spirit, Patti, and a bunch of sixteen-year-old guys brought me back to a life of obedience," he said.

In Houston, Vince started his first job with Sun Microsystems. As a recent college graduate, he set his sights on a $30,000 salary—but for the first six years after college he made over $300,000 a year. In his astounding success, he began to get overly impressed with himself.

Six years and three children later, he left to work briefly at the family business before starting his own software company. The company was just beginning to thrive when Vince discovered his partner, also a church deacon, had stolen the payroll taxes several quarters in a row. On that same day, Vince locked the doors and walked away from the company. "For three years, I hadn't taken a salary. I'd put everything I had made at Sun into this company, and all of a sudden, there was no company and I'd lost everything," Vince said.

The day Vince pulled the plug on the company's life support, he had to attend a friend's funeral. There he ran into the headhunter who had been after him to interview at a wealth management firm. Four days later, Vince was interviewing for the job, and two weeks after that he was living in New York City and beginning a new career.

Vince loved learning the new skills, but there were parts of the job he had a difficult time accepting. "You have to look at people the way the world does," Vince said. "You walk into a room and look for the dollar signs floating over people's heads. Whoever has the biggest dollar sign is the most important person in the room. Advisors try to promote themselves as the smartest guy in the industry and you spend all your time trying to get into the circles with wealthy people and their centers of influence." Eventually, Vince decided there had to be a better way.

WHEN YOUR WIFE IS FIFTY-FIVE

After three and a half years with that firm, Vince transitioned to the Houston office of a premier wealth management firm where he was blessed with co-workers who were believers. While there, Vince built up a list of seventy clients and had $98 million in assets under management. (In the wealth management industry, $100 million in assets under management is the proof you have "made it.") However, Vince was still unsure if this career was for him. "Just looking for rich people and trying to get them to give me their money wasn't fulfilling," he said.

Everything changed when Vince attended a Generous Giving conference where he heard a story and a statistic that challenged the way he viewed his life and career. In one session, Dixie Fraley told the story of her husband's death in the same plane crash that killed golfer Payne Stewart. Dixie's husband, Robert, was a sports agent whose job was to make sure his clients' assets and accounts were well managed.

One day, a friend challenged Robert: "Have you done the same for your wife as you do for your clients? If something happens to you, will your wife be prepared to step into your shoes? Will she even know who to call?" That started a yearlong process of gathering all their financial information and assembling a team—an attorney, accountant, investment advisor, their pastor, and "Dandy Don" Meredith for relationships. Every year they would gather as a team and review everything—wills, trusts, financial plans, budgets, and goals for giving and serving. Just days after Robert's death, Dixie met with this personal board of advisors where they grieved together and agreed on a plan to help Dixie move forward.

At the Generous Giving conference, Dixie said, "Men, whatever you are dealing with personally or corporately right now, if you die, that is what we will be dealing with tomorrow." Another speaker shared the statistic that the average age a woman is widowed in the United States is fifty-five years old. So, any man whose wife is fifty-five or older is living on borrowed time.

> Any man whose wife is fifty-five or
> older is living on borrowed time.

When he heard Dixie's story and this statistic, Vince realized he was a bad husband and advisor because he had not prepared his own wife for the day he wouldn't come home, nor was he talking to his clients about the most important issues in their lives. This was a wakeup call—a new perspective on how he could give. For Vince, the giving journey was about to continue in an entirely new way.

ON GIVING AWAY CLIENTS

About a year after the Generous Giving conference, Vince was working with a very difficult client who had no peace or joy; everything in the markets and in life terrified him. "Every day I had to talk him off the ledge and assure him that he was doing the right thing," Vince said. Even Vince's manager repeatedly challenged him to fire the client. But he was reluctant because this was his largest client by far.

Finally, Vince told the client that their relationship was no longer working. The relief of losing the client was so great that Vince decided to keep cutting clients who were similar. He said, "I want to work with people who exhibit the fruit of the Spirit, particularly peace and joy. If you don't have peace, I can't make you rich enough to find it. If you don't have joy, I can't double your wealth to double your joy. My job cannot be just to make people richer—I have to strive to help them use money in their lives to reach their true goals: their relationship with their wife, their relationship with their kids, their walk with Christ, their involvement in the community."

Over the next two years, Vince was in continual prayer as he cut his client list. Some people he felt he shouldn't be working with; others were uncomfortable with the new direction he had taken. He went from seventy clients to only sixteen.

At first, Vince was worried. "It wasn't as if I was at the top of my industry with the luxury to slash assets without consequences. In fact, I thought I was probably going to get fired as my assets under management were cut in half. However, God made it clear that it was Him at work and not me. He began to shower my clients with blessings. For example, I had a client with five million and I thought she would always have five million. A year later, she was a twenty-two million dollar client. God began to grow and multiply my practice even though I didn't add any new clients."

LESSONS OF THE BUMPY ROAD

Today, Vince has a newfound freedom in speaking with his clients. For example, he will ask them, "What has wealth achieved for you?" If they answer "security," he will introduce them to a couple who lost their daughter. If they answer "comfort," he will share the story of a couple whose children have wandered far from their desires for them.

Now, when Vince meets with prospects looking for a new advisor, his first statement is this: "I'm a financial advisor who thinks money isn't very important. In fact, I think wealth may be more dangerous to your family than a blessing. My role in your life is to help you keep money in its proper role—to not find security in it, because there is no security in an account number. Not to be in love with it, because it will deceive you and it will not love you back. My role is to help you pursue your true goals. I know the man you claim to be, and I'm going to walk alongside you to help you remain that man because money will change who you are. The only way to keep that from happening is to hold wealth with an open hand."

> I'm a financial advisor who thinks
> money isn't very important.

Vince will quickly tell you that when God took away his family's financial reserve, their cushion, that was the day when God worked most effectively in his life. Everything was better: his marriage, his relationships, his ministry, and his personal walk with Christ. He said, "God will put us in a place where we can hear His voice. For me, that meant taking me to a place of great financial insecurity. And I thank Him deeply that He loved me enough to do it."

Often, we equate generosity as giving away money. Certainly a part of generosity is giving money, but it's so much more than that. Sometimes it's about giving up your reputation—being called a "Jesus freak"—so that the cause of Christ advances and not your own. Sometimes it's about giving up your pride so you can learn who is really in control of your life. God gives us an opportunity to lose things we think are important to gain Him. Sometimes it means giving up clients—giving them away to others—even if there's a cost.

In the end, Vince's journey of generosity is a bumpy road. "My story isn't the guy who wrote the hundred million dollar check or built an orphanage in Africa—many other people have greater capacity to give larger financial amounts. My life is about my relationships with family, friends, and clients; my desire to be faithful—the widow's mite is such a huge part of my story—and my time as a Young Life leader. I think the most eternally meaningful and rewarding thing I've done is thirty-plus years of hanging out with teenage guys and sharing the Gospel."

YOUR STORY:

1. One of Vince's favorite Scripture passages to share with clients is Deuteronomy 8, particularly verse 18: "You shall remember the Lord your God, for it is He who gives you power to get wealth...." Read Deuteronomy 8 and prayerfully reflect on it. How has your standard of living made God seem unnecessary or uninvolved in your life? What can you do to remember God again?

2. What did you think when you read that fifty-five is the average age American women are widowed? If this is the time you or your spouse might have left, how will you prepare, not only financially but also for eternity? Are your home affairs in order? Is your career having the Kingdom influence you want it to?

3. As Vince has been faithful to God's call on his life, his remaining clients have been blessed, not only financially but also as they are challenged to live for lasting value. While you may not be a financial advisor, what questions can you ask to encourage others to see wealth in its proper role? What blessings have you seen come from faithful living?

4. What do you think about Vince's claim that wealth may be more dangerous to your family than a blessing? What accountability do you have to ensure you stay committed to your values and remain the person you want to be despite your financial status?

DAYTON MOORE
Kansas City Royals (Kansas City, MO)

CHAPTER 12

FAITH, FAMILY, AND BASEBALL

"I never intended to be the general manager of a major league baseball team," Dayton Moore said. But in May 2006, as an act of faith, that is the position Dayton took with the Kansas City Royals.

A LEGACY OF GENEROSITY

Born in Wichita, Kansas, Dayton grew up as a baseball fanatic. His baseball heroes were George Brett and Pete Rose. Every possible moment, he had a bat and ball in his hands—baseball was his life and his passion. Most of his conversations with his grandmother centered on his boyhood team, the Kansas City Royals.

Dayton's own family is a story of resiliency. His father grew up poor and was placed in an orphanage before returning to live with an abusive stepfather. He had to learn how to survive. The challenges of his boyhood could have produced two kinds of people—either one resentful and bitter, or one humble and gentle. Dayton's father chose the latter.

As an adult, Dayton's father worked in the aviation industry, which meant he moved around often and worked long hours. Aside from Wichita, they also lived in Florida, Tennessee, New York, and Illinois. In spite of all this, Dayton's dad made sure to spend time with his family. He would often take his boys to the hangar where they would work on planes together. Occasionally, Dayton and his brother would get strapped into the back of a plane while his dad and a friend flew tests. "That was so valuable—getting to work with my dad," Dayton said.

Dayton's father also made sure his sons knew how to serve. "I saw a model of generosity in my father," Dayton said as he recalled how his father made him and his brother shovel the sidewalks of elderly neighbors, rake mounds of leaves, and mow grass for them. "As a kid, I always thought we had enough grass to mow in our own yard!" He admired the fact that even though his dad was raised in an orphanage, he always treated people with respect and humility. "One of the big lessons he taught me was that life is a privilege and I should treat each job like it was my last."

> Life is a privilege and I should treat
> each job like it was my last.

OUR SUCCESS IS TIED TOGETHER

Dayton applied those lessons to baseball, and by high school he had earned a scholarship to play at Garden City Community College as a shortstop and second baseman. Away from home for the first time, he was confronted with a newfound freedom to come and go as he pleased. That freedom led him to make mistakes in his personal life that pricked his conscience. More importantly, it led him to challenge what he believed.

In third grade, Dayton had prayed the sinner's prayer, but by the time he reached college, baseball was his god. His team and winning were everything to him, which is why he was frustrated when his teammates made poor life choices that affected the team. He began attending a Bible study with his teammates as a way to rally everyone around a bigger cause and keep them focused. He realized that the idea of being a "team" was crucial and "our success was tied together." Also, his study of God's Word was a way for him to begin to lead himself, but it also produced something much deeper in him—a real and profound faith.

His journey of faith continued as he began playing at George Mason University. After graduating in 1989, he went undrafted by the Major Leagues and signed with an independent league. "After I was cut in spring training, it became pretty apparent that my career was in coaching," he said. From 1990 to 1994, he was the assistant baseball coach at George Mason.

During these years, his relationship with a young lady named Marianne Bixler began to blossom. His marriage proposal was couched with a baseball disclaimer—he had a passion to be a college coach, he wasn't going to make a lot of money, and he was likely to be fired a few times. Faced with such a promising future, Marianne chose her young man of passion and vision. In 1992, they were married.

AN UNEXPECTED CAREER

As a result of his college baseball coaching experience, scouts with professional baseball teams began to ask him to consider a career as a baseball scout. He turned down every one of these offers because he wanted to continue coaching college baseball: "My desire was to be part of taking a group of thirty to thirty-five young men and seeing if I could be part of molding them into a team. I liked the idea of doing life together and instilling a set of values."

However, there was one scout who wouldn't take no for an answer. Roy Clark was a fabled and respected scout with the Atlanta Braves. He pushed Dayton to at least go to Atlanta for an interview. When the Braves offered Dayton a position as an area scout, he agreed to take the job. He told Marianne that he only wanted to stay for four years before returning to college coaching. Two years later, in 1996, Dayton was offered a job as the Assistant Director of Scouting in Atlanta. He never planned to consider the position, but at the time he was living in Washington, D.C. and just making $27,000 as an area scout.

Also, Marianne had given birth to their first child, Ashley, eight months earlier. Before their marriage, they had committed to letting Marianne stay home with their children, especially with the demands of baseball coaching. But with his current salary and the cost of living in D.C., they needed two incomes. The promotion to Assistant Director of Scouting came with an $8,000 raise, so they made the decision to move to Atlanta. However, Dayton still thought he would eventually return to the college game.

By 1999, he was promoted to Assistant Director of Player Development. In 2000, he became the International Director of Scouting before becoming the Director of Player Personnel in 2002. By 2004, he was named as the top general manager prospect by Baseball America. In 2005, the same publication rated him as a Top 10 Up-and-Coming Power Brokers in Major League Baseball. Also in 2005, the Mid-Atlantic Scouts Association named him as their Executive of the Year.

By the fall of 2005, he was getting inquiries from other teams for general manager positions. In November of that same year, he interviewed with the Boston Red Sox to be their general manager, but withdrew his name from consideration. "I was content to remain with the Braves—being a general manager was not my passion," he said.

GIVING BACK IN KANSAS CITY

In 2006, Dayton interviewed with the Kansas City Royals and was impressed by David and Dan Glass and their desire to build a model organization. Initially, Dayton didn't think he could take the role because he wasn't like other general managers. After much prayer and seeking counsel from his spiritual mentor Tim Cash, he believed God was asking him to take a risk even though it was uncomfortable, to take the job, and to see if he could build a culture of servant-leaders.

In reflecting upon his dizzying ride up the Major League ladder, it would be easy to brag. However, Dayton's perspective is different: "As I got into my faith walk, I realized I wasn't any more special than the next guy. I have these opportunities because God has opened the doors. And it's a tremendous blessing to work in baseball because I've loved it since I was little."

There is a second secret as well. "Marianne and I became regular givers when we moved to Atlanta, and that's when my career began to take off," Dayton said. He is quick to say he doesn't believe in giving to get—it is just what happened for him. "My dad always taught us that everything belongs to God and that you can't out-give God," Dayton said. "This isn't my money, and this isn't my team."

Through the example of his father and his own experiences, Dayton continues to give. In 2013, he established the C You in the Major Leagues Foundation. His primary goal is to grow the foundation to help families in crisis, Christian organizations, and youth baseball players. "I knew it would be important to give back to Kansas City and use the platform I've been given to reach people," he said.

That desire to give back is reflected in the mission and culture he seeks to bring to the Kansas City Royals: "To build an organization that every parent would be proud to have their son a part of." Philippians 2:3-4 is one of his theme verses: "Do nothing from selfish ambition or conceit, but in humility count others more significant than yourselves. Let each of you look not only to his own interests, but also to the interests of others." After all, Dayton knows that in baseball culture—where everyone is already passionate, smart, and hard working—the only way to stand out is to care more than anyone else.

The only way to stand out is to care more than anyone else.

As he has grown older, Dayton realizes that the challenges of life don't get any easier or more comfortable. But he also realizes the struggles of life are also a blessing. "My father died of colon cancer at age forty-nine," Dayton said, "but I was privileged to put everything on hold and be there with him. So many people came to his funeral because they respected the man he was. My mother died of cancer at sixty-nine, and I had the privilege of leading her to the Lord before she passed. And when my daughter Ashley suffered a near-fatal brain aneurysm at age fourteen, I watched her respond with such kindness and grace even though she was in tremendous pain…I'm not sure how people make it in life without a faith walk."

As Dayton's story illustrates, it is a recognition of faith and a family woven together that makes our lives rich and allows us to give to others.

YOUR STORY:

1. Despite the difficult childhood of Dayton's father, he still chose to love well. This legacy still affects his children and all the people they have influenced. After you are gone, what do you want your children to be saying about your legacy?

2. At what point in your life did your giving become consistent? What impact did that have on you? And if it's never been consistent, how might you begin that journey today?

3. Dayton said he obtained the position he has not because he's special but because God opened doors for him. What doors has God opened in your life? How are you using those doors to become more Christlike or to advance the Kingdom?

FAMILY GENEROSITY

Beware lest you say in your heart, "My power and the might of my hand have gotten me this wealth." You shall remember the Lord your God, for it is He who gives you power to get wealth, that He may confirm His covenant that He swore to your fathers, as it is this day.

—DEUTERONOMY 8:17-18

You shall therefore lay up these words of mine in your heart and in your soul, and you shall bind them as a sign on your hand, and they shall be as frontlets between your eyes. You shall teach them to your children, talking of them when you are sitting in your house, and when you are walking by the way, and when you lie down, and when you rise. You shall write them on the doorposts of your house and on your gates, that your days and the days of your children may be multiplied in the land that the Lord swore to your fathers to give them, as long as the heavens are above the earth.

—DEUTERONOMY 11:18-21

DAVID GREEN
Hobby Lobby (Oklahoma City, OK)

GENEROSITY

CHAPTER 13

A PURPOSE FOR
THE MERCHANT

What does it mean to be doing the Lord's work? David Green, founder and CEO of Hobby Lobby, wrestled with that question for a long time. He came from a family of preachers—his father was a pastor and David's two brothers and two sisters either became pastors or married pastors.

Unlike his siblings, David wasn't a big fan of high school. He got his big break when he discovered there was a class called Distributive Education that allowed him to go to school for half a day and then work the other half. He began working at TG&Y, a local five-and-dime, where he discovered his two great loves—his wife, Barbara, and his love for retail.

However, compared to his siblings in ministry, David felt like the black sheep of the family. By the time he was twenty-one, David was a store manager with TG&Y and working his way through the ranks. As he and Barbara began having children, he found the hours were too long. Sometimes, it was all he could do to make it home in time to tuck his two boys into bed. This early experience would serve to influence him much later when he had his own store.

TAKING A RISK

As David moved up the ladder at TG&Y, he began to have a desire to own his own store. At the age of twenty-eight, he and a partner invested $600 into a wood-cutting machine with which they could make picture frames. His two boys, Mart and Steve, got paid seven cents a frame for assembling them.

In 1972, they opened a three hundred-square-foot retail space with an additional three hundred square feet of backroom inventory. The early sales were positive. David said, "I never went into the arts-and-crafts business expecting to get wealthy. It was simply a way to make a modest living to support my family and to put food on the table."

Initially, when the first store opened, Barbara worked in the store without pay. David continued to work at TG&Y while the fledgling business got off the ground. But sales progressed, and they moved to a second location. As the business grew, David and Barbara took the risk and David quit his job at TG&Y to concentrate on growing their own business.

THE HUMILITY LESSON

The early days were fresh and fun as the business continued to grow. Hobby Lobby, as the business came to be called, added new stores and new locations. Their apparent success was about to be challenged, however.

Like most businesses, Hobby Lobby used a line of credit to purchase its inventory. They began to take on some higher-end inventory that started moving slowly. That slower-moving inventory coupled with a downturn in the oil economy produced a ripple effect. Banks and creditors became very nervous about high levels of leverage and began squeezing Hobby Lobby for payment. On the other hand, the downturn also produced dampened sales. It was the perfect storm.

As the creditors pressed in, David found himself with nowhere to turn. Many days he would crawl under his desk and cry out to God in prayer. He feared losing the business, so he called his family together to deliver the grim news. In a moment for which he is forever grateful, his oldest son, Mart, told him, "Don't worry, Dad. Our trust is in the Lord."

Don't worry, Dad. Our trust is in the Lord.

Eventually, the cloud began to clear—miraculously. Sales picked up and the company survived. But it was a deeply humbling time, and David acknowledged, "My pride had gotten in the way, and God seemed to say to me, 'You think you're so big; well, here it is.'"

David's second son, Steve, also played a role in the company's development. After studying the Scriptures, Steve invited David and Barbara over for dinner. Steve shared from Scripture how a borrower is always a slave to the lender, and encouraged the business to get out of debt. David took the advice and began moving their company toward debt-free status.

THE MERCHANT'S PURPOSE

From his childhood days, David remembered his parents' staunch devotion to God and his mother's careful attention to tithing. His mother would keep track of everything given to them, including food supplies given as an offering. Then she would make gifts out of everything given to them.

A familiar refrain from a poem by C.T. Studd, echoed by his mother, was an embroidered picture in their family home:

Only one life, 'twill soon be past,
Only what's done for Christ will last.

Even as his business grew, his mother would still encourage David by asking, "What are you doing for the Lord?" The answer to that question came in a surprising way.

In 1979, David attended an international missions conference in Tennessee where missionaries from all over the world gave presentations. David remembered how his mother had always given to international missions. As he flew home after the meetings ended, David was reminded of one speaker who had shared the need for more printed material in his particular mission field. David sensed a quiet voice in his spirit saying, "You need to give thirty thousand dollars for literature." The number was far bigger than he imagined, and he certainly didn't have it immediately available, but David put four checks of $7,500 each, post-dated over the course of four months, in an envelope. He prayed over the checks and mailed them to Tennessee.

Upon receiving the checks, the church official told David, "The very day your letter was postmarked, four missionaries to Africa had a special prayer meeting for literature funds. Looks like God answered their prayer!"

This experience had a profound impact on David. "My longstanding uneasiness about not going in the ministry like all my brothers and sisters went away." David realized, "Maybe God has a purpose for a merchant after all."

THE RISING TIDE

Today, Hobby Lobby has over five hundred stores in forty-eight states. Sales have topped $3 billion annually with more stores planned. As David realized his purpose, he also realized that he was a minister, at least of sorts, to his employees.

Hobby Lobby closes at 8 p.m. every night so his employees can at least be at home with their children. They are closed on Sunday so employees can attend church if they choose. As a company, they've also been careful to provide educational programs around financial literacy so employees can make wise financial decisions. Hobby Lobby has also consistently paid the highest minimum wage of any company—today they pay a $15 an hour minimum wage for full-time employees.

As the employees have been rewarded, they've responded with great care for their work. And the company has flourished. "Hobby Lobby is a place for people to make their home just a little bit better," David said.

Hobby Lobby's growth has allowed them to expand their giving as well. Each year Hobby Lobby seeks to give 50 percent of its profit to Kingdom work. As David has noted: "We've set out to work with organizations that directly tell people about Christ, from global ministries such as Every Home for Christ, to our local rescue mission. In this way, we hope to keep Hobby Lobby on track as God's company, not ours. We want the company to continue for decades, even centuries, as an ongoing source of financial fuel for God's work around the world." They take special joy in the fact that their three children have continued in the business as well as some of their grandchildren.

> We want the company to continue for decades, even centuries, as an ongoing source of financial fuel for God's work around the world.

Each month, the family gathers together to make giving decisions. David, his wife, Barbara, and their three children—Mart, Steve, and Darsee—are all involved. They've been able to be very creative as a family, including projects like the following:

- They've bought buildings for Christ-centered ministries. Their son Steve has led the real estate area of the business and ministry.

- Their oldest son, Mart, put the story of Nate Saint and the Waodoni Tribe on film in the documentary *Beyond the Gates of Splendor* and the movie *End of the Spear*.

- They estimate they've reached nearly 2 billion people with the Gospel of Christ through the ministries they support like Every Home for Christ and One Hope.

- They have been active in promoting Bible translation and the digitization of Scripture through Every Tribe Every Nation.

- At Christmas and Easter, Hobby Lobby sponsors full-page ads that announce the message of the Savior in newspapers around the country. Their daughter Darsee leads the graphic arts aspect of their business.

- Their grandchildren participate in giving with a giving fund set up through the National Christian Foundation. They make quarterly decisions on where to give.

Perhaps their most aggressive work currently is creating a cultural conversation around truth by establishing The Museum of the Bible. This effort is led by Steve, their second son. The museum will feature Bible artifacts from around the world and be an interactive experience centered on the stories of the Bible, the history of the Bible, and the impact of the Bible. Based in Washington, D.C., it will be coupled with traveling exhibits, a Bible curriculum, and a collegiate scholars program.

David said, "It was not until my late thirties that I discovered the joy of giving to God's work as I came to realize its lasting value. I believe my responsibility to handle my company's assets is directly tied to God's endeavors in the world. He has asked folks like you and me to think like God thinks about resources so He can advance His priorities. Through the efforts of the company God has allowed us to build, I want as many people as possible to know Christ as Savior."

YOUR STORY:

1. What does it mean to be doing the Lord's work? For David, this was a long process to discover what that meant for him personally. What does it mean for you to be doing the Lord's work? Take some time to reflect on your journey toward understanding this.

2. One reason David has made business decisions like closing his stores at 8 p.m. is because he remembers what it was like to work as an employee. How can you discover and feel the pain points of people around you? How can you find generous ways to serve people at those places?

3. David's son Steve helped convict him that "the borrower is the slave of the lender" (Proverbs 22:7). What do you think about this principle? How might becoming debt-free give you the freedom to pursue greater generosity and freedom?

4. The Greens have many opportunities for their children and grandchildren to get involved with giving as a family. While this will look different for every family, how can you open the doors to discuss and practice family generosity?

**CLIFF BENSON JR. AND
CLIFF BENSON III**
American Homesmith (Raleigh, NC)

CHAPTER 14

BOOKS, BUILDERS, AND OUR 100 PERCENT

It's not easy for a family with a hundred-year-old tradition to change quickly. But that's just what happened to the Benson family after reading two books and listening to a CD.

THE FAMILY BUSINESS

In 1922, Cliff Benson Jr.'s great-uncle started Carolina Builders Corporation, a building supply business for professional homebuilders and contractors. The business was handed down to Cliff's father, and then Cliff Jr. bought it from his father in the early 1980s.

Cliff Jr. grew up in a hard-working family who attended a Methodist church and gave because it was the right thing to do. Cliff always planned on working in the family business, which is precisely what he did after his college graduation in 1964. He had a starting salary of $100 a week, but over the next twenty years the business grew ten-fold or more. By the mid-70s, the Raleigh-based business had expanded to many other North Carolina locations.

"While this is contradictory to a lot of things you'll hear," Cliff Jr. said, "I learned early that we really didn't have to worry too much about the bottom line. All we worried about was doing things the way they were supposed to be done. That way, the bottom line took care of itself. If we were good operators, we'd be fine—and that's what happened."

Then, in the summer of 1985, an English company walked in and offered to buy the business. This offer was completely unsolicited; the business was not for sale. They closed on the offer in January 1986. Cliff Jr. stayed on for two more years before hiring someone to replace him as president. In 1987, he left with "absolutely no regrets at all."

SPENDING AFTER SELLING

After Cliff left, he played a lot of golf and began investing, particularly in real estate. Six years later, he started a family office. At first, it was a loose organization for personal investing that morphed into something more formal with both a nonprofit and a business side. He had seen the mistakes other families made after selling a company, particularly as related to spending, and did not want his family to make the same mistakes now that they had extra cash. However, he didn't follow his own advice.

"I bought a big boat. I bought a plane. I bought a house in Florida. Then Business 101 kicked in concerning cash flow, so I sold a big boat, a plane, and a house in Florida," Cliff Jr. said. "It didn't make any sense. Some things are better to rent than own. After you've sold a company, do everything very carefully. Just put the money somewhere safe and figure out what you're going to do instead of making quick, emotional moves."

"Yes, don't do anything for a year," his son Cliff Benson III agreed. "No big decisions quickly."

THE NEXT GENERATION'S STORY

Cliff Jr.'s son, Cliff III, grew up going to church sporadically with his family but didn't really enjoy it. "We knew the right thing to do, but we lived more by the moral code than the biblical code," he said. However, when Cliff III was sixteen, his family began attending a new church where the Gospel was clearly presented. "I heard the Gospel and was compelled to respond, but I resisted and didn't respond. When I went to college, I put any faith thoughts out of my mind."

Cliff III was a sophomore in college when the family company sold in 1986. While he had planned to work at the company, he thought it would be easy enough to find another job. But he wasn't expecting the career turn his life would take.

During Christmas break his senior year of college, he played golf for the first time in his life and really enjoyed it. After he graduated, he began golfing every day as he decided he could enjoy the summer before starting the job hunt in the fall. But by the end of the summer, he had improved his golf game to the point where he was shooting par. That year, in 1989, he moved to Florida and went pro. For the next eleven years, he played professional golf and tried to get onto the PGA Tour.

While on tour, Cliff III developed a passion for reading, especially as he traveled and stayed in hotels. (He called this "the Lord's sense of humor," because in college he used to pride himself on the fact that he had never read a book—a fact made possible with the help of *Masterplots'* book summaries.) His maternal grandmother, the spiritual matriarch of the family, was also an avid reader, so she began sending him books. Among the classic novels and literature, she also slipped in some C.S. Lewis, G.K. Chesterton, and other Christian classics.

Then, in 1990, his father got involved with Bible Study Fellowship in Raleigh. As he and his dad discussed what they were learning, Cliff III decided to find out what the Bible contained. "I read an NIV Life

Application Bible literally cover to cover," Cliff III said. "Somewhere in the New Testament, I surrendered and put my faith in Christ. That was three years after I married and a month before our first child was born."

THE CD THAT BEGAN IT ALL

In 2000, Cliff III left his golf career and came to work for the family office. Somewhere between 2003 and 2004, a friend gave them a Generous Giving CD. As they listened to the CD, it challenged them to consider the biblical view of generosity for the first time. At that point in their lives, they had not heard of giving more than the tithe. From there, *The Treasure Principle* by Randy Alcorn and *The Eternity Portfolio* by Alan Gotthardt furthered their understanding of generosity, both personally and with their business interests.

Cliff III said, "The two ideas that stood out to me were, 'Where your treasure is, there your heart will be also,' and 'You can't take it with you, but you can send it on ahead.' Also, as we got into the Word, we saw that the heart of God is generosity: 'For God so loved the world that He gave….' We had to wrestle through that because it's not purely about financial giving, but it's about your heart. It's finances and everything else."

Previously, Cliff III said they were "tickled tithers"—someone who tithes, then pats himself on the back and feels good for doing the right thing. As they learned about generosity, Cliff III said, "It became clear *why* we're supposed to be generous and why we should continue on even more so. It's not about giving God His ten percent. God owns it all. It is about figuring out what He wants me to do with the 100 percent He has entrusted to me."

> It is about figuring out what He wants me to do with the 100 percent He has entrusted to me.

GROWING GENEROSITY WITH THE FAMILY

As the family continued to grow in faith, they began to reconsider their giving through their family foundation. When the business sold, they had established the foundation simply because that was the right thing to do. The foundation gave the IRS-mandated 5 percent a year, but it remained fairly idle. Now they gathered the family together and created a giving statement. As they went through the process, they discovered their family was passionate about children, Scripture translation, and religious liberties.

"We tried to narrow down what we felt God was calling us to do, and then became proactive in finding things that fit where we were called," Cliff III said. "As we became more intentional, we dramatically reduced the number of ministries we supported while increasing the amounts we gave to the remaining ones," Cliff Jr. added. "We went from being a shotgun to a rifle."

Aside from the foundation, the Bensons have also tried different things to encourage their family's involvement in giving. Cliff III has taken each of his children on one-on-one trips to see God's work worldwide. "That seems to bear as much fruit as telling them about giving," he said. "Seeing what God is doing in different parts of the world is very powerful. It gives us a very cool perspective of God's heart for the whole world, not just our part of it."

This past Christmas, Cliff Jr. set up a giving fund for his six grandchildren in each of their names. "How it works and whether it sticks or not, we'll have to see over time," he said. "But recently I saw the first gift go out from one of them. At least they know it's there, and we'll just see where it leads."

LEADING OTHERS AND MOVING FORWARD

The Bensons also find themselves in the sometimes-uncomfortable position of being generosity ambassadors because promoting generosity is not the easiest thing for them. "You have to fight really hard to get past your pride and self-righteousness," Cliff Jr. said. "But when you're passionate about something, it becomes part of your normal conversations."

As they talk to others about generosity, and sometimes even load entire buses to take people to Generous Giving conferences, Cliff III said, "Really deep down, you're hoping they'll have the same experience we did, because it's a really fun journey. However, the results have nothing to do with us. It's like evangelizing—whether the person changes or comes to the Lord is not our job. We just try to lead by example and let God take it from there."

Looking ahead, the Bensons are excited about giving more. Five years ago, they started a homebuilding company with the intent of giving away 50 percent of its earnings. They have the same goal for any new company they might start. "I think that's what excites us," Cliff III said. "With starting a business, we're making money so we can give it away."

Cliff Jr. agreed: "All we want to do is build quality homes, have satisfied customers, love on our employees, and make money so we can give more away. One thing that's changed my thought process is hearing about a guy in Texas who drew a line in the sand regarding his net worth. He decided his net worth would never go over a hundred million dollars. And then he began giving away thirty to forty million a year. I've drawn my line and encouraged all my friends to do the same. Your line could be one million or a hundred million dollars—it is completely between you and the Lord—but just draw one."

> Your line could be $1 million or $100 million—it is completely between you and the Lord—but just draw one.

"In Scripture, it talks about laying up treasure in Heaven and taking hold of life that is truly life," Cliff III said. "It is fun. It *is* more blessed to give than receive. That verse illustrates my heart—it's the eternal perspective."

"I forgot to say that," Cliff Jr. agreed. "That part of it, having fun, is a *big* deal. Generosity is fun! There is no way you can know how much fun it is until you're there. When you're spending on yourself, the joy part passes quickly, but the joy of giving and its eternal rewards—that lasts a long time."

YOUR STORY:

1. After coming into money (whether through the sale of a company, a major bonus, an inheritance, etc.), the Bensons' advice is to slow down and not make any hasty, emotional purchases. Should this happen to you, what is your plan of action? What can you do to ensure you make wise, God-honoring decisions during that time?

2. The five influences that have greatly challenged the Bensons in their generosity journey are the Bible, a Generous Giving CD, *The Treasure Principle* (Alcorn), *How Much Land Does a Man Need?* (Tolstoy), and *The Eternity Portfolio* (Gotthardt). Choose two books or CDs about generosity to go through. Summarize what you learned from them with your family.

3. The Bensons said they used to be "tickled tithers" who didn't understand biblical generosity but felt good because they did the "right thing" by giving 10 percent of their income to the work of God. However, it's not about percentages and formulas; God wants to know what you're doing with 100 percent. Review your family or business budget without regard to percentages and pray about how God is leading you to handle your 100 percent.

4. Generosity can be a difficult and sensitive subject to discuss with others. However, the Bensons learned the results are not up to them—it is God's work. How can you encourage and challenge others to discover generosity while trusting that God is still at work in their lives?

GENEROSITY

BOB HODGDON
Hodgdon Powder Company
(Shawnee, KS)

CHAPTER 15

GUNPOWDER AND GENEROSITY

Sometimes it takes an explosion to change your life. When he was thirty-eight, Bob Hodgdon's gunpowder business literally blew up. However, the consequences were far more than Bob could ever imagine.

BEGINNINGS

Bob was nine when his father, Bruce Hodgdon, a gas service salesman, bought his first fifty thousand pounds of World War II surplus government gunpowder. Bob, his older brother, and their mother were the first employees of B.E. Hodgdon, Inc. (now Hodgdon Powder Company), a manufacturer and supplier of propellant to the sporting ammunition community.

The business did very well and paid its startup loans within four months of opening. Despite the company's success, Bob's father kept the family on a tight budget. Bob's mother was a generous person, but his father did not enjoy giving to the church. So his mother creatively skimped in other areas of her budget so she had enough to give to the church and to help others.

After Bob graduated from college, he and his brother, J.B., went into the business and eventually became the owners and managers.

A LIFE-CHANGING EXPLOSION

In 1974, Bob met Dan Pawlak, a young pyrotechnician who did special effects for the movies. One of Dan's friends had been killed in a black powder explosion, so Dan wanted to make a safer form of black powder… and he succeeded.

The first thing Dan asked when he met Bob was, "Are you a Christian?" Bob had attended mainline churches and knew some Scripture, so he thought, "I'm not a Hindu or a Muslim, so sure, I'm a Christian." Within weeks, Dan and Bob established a good business relationship.

When Dan's product, which was being exclusively marketed by Hodgdon Powder Company, hit the market, it became the first commercially successful improvement to black powder since its invention in the 1200s. Bob visited the plant for the first time in early January 1977 where he stayed with Dan and his wife. Ten days later, on January 27, Dan and three others were killed in a plant explosion. Dan was just thirty years old.

Bob visited the plant's twisted wreckage in shock before attending four funerals in three days. But Dan had a policy of hiring all Christians, so these funerals were unlike anything Bob had ever experienced before—they were celebrations! Even Dan's young widow, with a toddler and a newborn, faced the future with optimism. With a softened heart, Bob returned home. Soon afterward, his sister-in-law invited him to church and, at the age of thirty-eight, Bob became a Christian.

BANKRUPTCY ATTORNEYS AND TITHING

Bob knew Christians tithed, and while he gave money to the church, he always had an excuse for why he couldn't quite give the tithe. After reading the Bible cover to cover four times, however, he began tithing.

Around the same time, the company ran into difficulty. They brought Dan's company back to Kansas, Bob's home. However, to get Dan's product back on the market, they had to build a new plant. Cost overruns, delays in production, two accidents, and the recall of a hundred thousand defective containers occurred before meaningful production. Most of all, the company was already in debt and the new plant shoved them further into debt. Bob and J.B. were advised to see bankruptcy attorneys.

Bob and J.B. refused the advice. Their banker and most of their lenders were friends and the debts were large enough that it would be very difficult for the lenders to survive should Bob declare bankruptcy. Bob could not see surviving financially himself while taking down other people. The next few years were a struggle, but Bob believes God honored their decision to refuse the lawyers' advice.

For the next four years, Bob and J.B. went without any income aside from the $10,000 a year inheritance their parents could provide each husband and wife. Finally, in 1990, the company paid off the industrial revenue bonds that financed the plant and they could breathe again.

Yet even through that difficult period, Bob continued to tithe faithfully. His faith was new, but his tithe was a sign and sacrifice showing the Lord he was serious about his faith commitment.

TURNING POINTS

As Bob continued to grow in his understanding of generosity, two things greatly shaped his viewpoint. First, someone gave him Larry Burkett's *Business by the Book* that contained lots of scriptural truth about generosity. One thing that stood out was that if your company is a C-corporation—which Bob's was—then your earnings and taxes are separate from the company. However, the company is accumulating earnings for your benefit, so you should also tithe on the company's income.

Bob and J.B. discussed it and decided it was the right thing to do. That same year, the company released a patented product, Pyrodex muzzle-loading pellets, that caught on like crazy. The company's earnings skyrocketed and made much more even after tithing.

However, Bob is careful to differentiate this from the prosperity Gospel that says one gives in order to get. He said, "You get blessed in lots of ways when you give—lots of ways—but not always financially. But we were blessed financially, so we were able to start a charitable foundation with those tithes."

> You get blessed in lots of ways when
> you give—lots of ways—
> but not always financially.

The other major influence on Bob's viewpoint was a limited edition Crown Financial Ministries study a friend taught to several couples. As Bob studied the Scripture the course presented, his heart changed. He said, "I finally got the message that it's not mine. We are stewards. We're here for the long haul."

FAMILY INVOLVEMENT

After the Crown class, Bob was so excited about generosity that he had to share it with his family. Up until this point, he and J.B. made all the giving decisions themselves. Initially, they had a company charitable foundation, but they ultimately switched to a giving fund with National Christian Foundation because it was easier to use.

Bob and J.B. decided to bring the entire family together (children and grandchildren) and involve them in giving. This practice has evolved to a formalized situation with a grant request form, a mission statement, and a set of guidelines. All family members are invited to the monthly meeting and children can vote once they turn eighteen. Generally, the foundation will not award a grant unless the vote is unanimous because they want to be united as a family.

They place special emphasis on startup or small ministries that do great work but need capital. They also heavily lean toward organizations that one or more of the family members either has a passion for it or is involved in giving his or her own time or money.

However, one of Bob's favorite gifts is a swimming pool he installed in his backyard in 1994 so his house could be a haven for his teenage children and their friends. Now that he has grandchildren, it is still a place for the family to hang out. He said, "I didn't build the pool for me. I'm the guy who has to clean it and treat it and keep it going. But it's been a blessing to the kids and a good investment in family togetherness. I think this fits under the general heading of generosity because one of my main priorities is family."

SACRIFICIAL GIVING AND GOD'S GENEROSITY

One of Bob's favorite stories is about God's generosity. His church started a building campaign to expand their crowded sanctuary, and Bob wanted to give sacrificially. Because he had significant financial means, he searched for something sacrificial to contribute.

He realized that every morning he made Suisse Mocha coffee, which is a candy coffee General Foods distributes. He calculated that if he gave up his morning coffee for the next three years (the length of the campaign), he'd be able to give an additional $780.

> If he gave up his morning coffee for the next three years (the length of the campaign), he'd be able to give an additional $780.

As Bob finished the last container of coffee in the house, he gave a five-minute speech at church because he was on the church's financial campaign committee. In the speech, he mentioned his decision to forgo his coffee.

Two days later, the phone rang. A woman asked if this was the Mr. Hodgdon who spoke at church because she had something for him. Later that evening, she came to his door with a box and introduced herself as a General Foods employee. And in that box was several months' supply of Bob's Suisse Mocha. Bob added, "And the strange thing is, I've never seen her or heard from her since. I've looked for her at every church service, but maybe it was one of God's angels. You just cannot out-give God."

FINAL THOUGHTS

As Bob considered what he has learned about generosity, he said, "Being generous is rewarding; it's fun. There's almost some selfishness in being generous and getting to enjoy seeing what is happening with your money. One of the things I really loved from that Crown study was this phrase, 'Debt is bad. Saving is good. Stuff is meaningless. Giving is fun.' And that is very true."

YOUR STORY:

1. Even during the four years Bob's business was struggling, he remained committed to generosity. Regardless of your current situation, how is God calling you to faithful stewardship?

2. Generosity often involves sacrifice, whether it is being sacrificial with your money or your morning Suisse Mocha coffee. List one thing you could do to practice sacrificial generosity: _____

3. For Bob, reading the Bible cover to cover, Larry Burkett's *Business by the Book,* and a Crown Financial study greatly shaped his understanding of generosity. What are three resources you could read or study to learn more about God's view of generosity?

   • _____

   • _____

   • _____

UNEXPECTED GENEROSITY

Truly, truly, I say to you, unless a grain of wheat falls into the earth and dies, it remains alone; but if it dies, it bears much fruit. Whoever loves his life loses it, and whoever hates his life in this world will keep it for eternal life. If anyone serves Me, he must follow Me; and where I am, there will My servant be also. If anyone serves Me, the Father will honor him.

—JOHN 12:24-26

Photo credit: Nancy Jo McDaniel

ORIGINAL ONE HUNDRED SHARES BOARD

ANNE IRWIN
One Hundred Shares (Atlanta, GA)

CHAPTER 16

GIVING CIRCLES AND SEEING MESSY

Anne Irwin was busy. Aside from being a wife and mother, she also owned and managed a thriving business. But one day she read a magazine article describing giving circles and how people pooled their money together to contribute to causes for greater impact. There were environmental giving circles, political circles, and women's health circles, but seemingly no circles for giving to Christian ministries. She thought someone ought to start a giving circle for local Christian ministries…but not her—she was too busy and had too little knowledge.

First Experiences

Growing up, Anne's father was on her church's financial committee. He found that it was difficult to get people to support the church. Much of the giving seemed done out of obligation and with reluctance because the church also financially supported political and activist causes with no correlation to the Gospel.

It was not until Anne was in college that she understood the meaning of Christianity and how to have a personal relationship with the God of the universe. She joined a campus ministry's Bible study that discussed many topics, including generosity and the scriptural reasons for it.

SEEDS OF AN IDEA

After Anne met her husband, she moved to Georgia where he was in graduate school for eight years. Even through the years when money was tight and her husband worked several jobs, the Irwins enjoyed giving. However, they typically gave smaller amounts to large organizations or missions groups. They knew their money was helping someone, but most of the time they had no firsthand knowledge of the money's effect. Plus, it often seemed like their meager amount could not possibly make a difference.

Then, in the early 2000s, Anne began seeing magazine articles about women's giving groups. She thought, "Someone should really start this for Christian women." Several years later, the nudge came: "Why don't you start a giving group?"

> Several years later, the nudge came: "Why don't you start a giving group?"

Anne protested internally. "I wrestled with myself because I was *so busy*. I thought, 'I couldn't possibly do it. A startup is hard and I don't have the time or knowledge for it.' So I kept trying to think of someone else who could do it."

When Anne finally realized she was supposed to start her own giving circle, she called a few close friends she felt were smart and would have a good understanding of whether this idea would work. Her friends' excitement was contagious and, within a month or two, they had a board of ten women committed to starting the circle. Each of the women on the board also said they knew an additional ten women who might be interested in participating. Within three months they had a hundred

women in their circle. The new giving circle, One Hundred Shares (www
.onehundredshares.org), was easy to start as a giving fund with the
National Christian Foundation.

SIMPLE MULTIPLICATION

One Hundred Shares is a simple idea designed to be replicated in
cities across the nation. There are no extravagant galas, coffees, or speakers that cost money and detract from what could be sent to ministries.
Each woman simply gives $1,000 a year. Ministries can submit grant
applications all year long and then the board selects four semi-finalists in
September. Site visits to the semi-finalists are set up and anyone who is a
member of the giving circle has an opportunity to attend. Board members
then vote to distribute the money either in one bulk amount or split it
between two ministries.

> The thing that excites me about
> One Hundred Shares is that we're
> multiplying people's money.

Anne said, "The thing that excites me about One Hundred Shares is
that we're multiplying people's money. A thousand dollars can be helpful, but there are so many great organizations where a larger monetary
boost would change their entire ministry. But if you have a hundred
women each giving a thousand dollars, that is one hundred thousand
dollars to share."

The beauty of One Hundred Shares is that it is very simple: just
give $1,000, go on a site visit if led, and see how God works. Anne said,
"And what happens is women go on these site visits and get excited about
becoming personally involved with a particular ministry. Regardless of
whether the giving circle ends up awarding a grant to that ministry, some
women start getting involved with their time."

SEEING GOD'S HEART

As Anne has continued to work with One Hundred Shares, she has seen more of God's heart, especially for the poor. She said, "Over and over again, in the strangest places in both the Old and New Testaments, you see God's concern for the poor. So visiting these ministries and seeing where our money might go has given me a completely different perspective on what other believers are doing and how effective they are. My favorite verse is Matthew 25:40, 'And the King will answer them, "Truly, I say to you, as you did it to one of the least of these my brothers, you did it to Me."' That is incredible motivation for giving."

To date, One Hundred Shares has given away over $800,000. So far, their focus, like Anne's passion, is the poor and underserved in their community. They have helped diverse ministries, ranging from those who rescue women from the sex trade, to providing air conditioning to the inner-city elderly, to sending urban children to summer camp.

One of Anne's favorite gifts was a van that transports women from a shelter to job interviews. It seemed like a simple gift, but it made a significant difference to the ministry because now the women do not have to worry about running into their pimps or drug dealers on public transportation.

LEAVING THE STANDS

One Hundred Shares also provides training and materials to start giving circles in other cities. Currently, besides the circle in Atlanta, there are also One Hundred Shares groups in Dallas, Houston, Fort Lauderdale, Tampa, and San Diego, along with several other cities that have expressed interest in starting one.

When asked what advice she would give to people unsure about starting a giving circle, Anne laughed as she said, "Don't do it!" She explained that without a calling, a passion, and the recognition that this could really make a difference, a giving circle becomes just another duty to accomplish.

However, passion can blossom and grow, especially when it is seen and experienced at the ground level. Anne saw a clear picture of this through a college football game. One night, the coach invited several people to watch the game on the field. Anne was completely shocked by the difference of watching football on the field as opposed to the stands.

High in the stands, it is easy to judge and make comments: "Why didn't the receiver catch that pass?" or "Why is the quarterback passing it over there? That other player was completely open!" But when you're on the field, you can't see it all. Anne said, "There's noise and there's yelling and the defensive linemen are trying to intimidate the quarterback. You wonder how the quarterback could ever see past the defensive line to the waiting receiver who is halfway down the field."

Anne related this to giving: "When you're in the 'stands,' it's very sterile, very clean. You write your donation checks, send them off, feel good about them, and then you leave the game. But when you get down on ground level, you see how messy and incredible it is, and you are amazed that anyone could ever come out of this whole. And when someone's life does change in the midst of the messiness, it is amazing because you know how hard it is to see there…. That's what giving is. It's a completely different game with a completely different appreciation when you get involved and see it at ground level."

YOUR STORY:

1. There are many reasons it can be difficult to get involved. For Anne, a major concern was her lack of time, but she was able to overcome it through the calling of God and friends' help. What things are hindering you from getting involved? List three steps you can take to address those challenges:

   • _____

   • _____

   • _____

2. One reason Anne enjoys One Hundred Shares is because it helps others multiply their giving. Where is an opportunity for you to multiply your giving or help others do the same?

3. Sometimes, the most difficult part is discerning where your passion is and where God might be calling you. What are some things you could ask, do, see, or experience to help you understand where God is leading you?

4. Generosity can be very "clean" when seen from the stands. While donations are usually necessary for a ministry's growth, how might God be calling you to get involved at the ground level?

GENEROSITY

**DEBBIE MASSEY AND
MICHELLE YORK**
Helping Hands Ministries
(Tallulah Falls, GA)

CHAPTER 17

THE WORK OF TRAGEDY, NEED, AND MIRACLES

The best stories. The worst stories. All at once. These are the stories of the joy of the giver and the joy and heartache of the recipient. That's the life of Debbie Massey and Michelle York every single day. It often looks like this: a distraught man calls and says in tension-filled words, "My brother-in-law was just in a car accident, and he's paralyzed and will never walk again. What do I do?"

As project coordinators for Helping Hands Ministries in Tallulah Falls, Georgia, Debbie and Michelle may have one of the best and one of the most difficult jobs. Most of their days are filled with interacting with individuals and families who have financial needs due to a medical crisis, job loss, family emergency, or educational expenses.

Helping Hands is a ministry that grants funds to individuals in need. Most often, they hear of needs through people who desire to give to others who are experiencing greater needs. Their ministry's thought is, "My excess is likely someone else's necessity."

A BOX OF LETTERS

One of Michelle's favorite stories is about a young woman we will call Shelby. When Shelby graduated from college, she was thousands of dollars in student loan debt and struggling to manage on her own.

When she was young, life seemed to be perfect: a mom and dad, a brother, a dog, and even a white picket fence. When she was thirteen, however, it all fell apart. Shelby's dad left and her mother struggled taking on the full responsibility for the family. Her family moved from their house into a small apartment while her mother worked full-time just to survive. Shelby went into a deep depression. But it was through that season of depression that she was led to her heavenly Father.

As the years went by, Shelby continued to write letters to her dad in an attempt to build a bridge to him. One day, she received a box in the mail. It contained every letter she had written…all unopened. The moment she opened the box, Shelby said peace surrounded her. It was like God said it was enough.

Several years later, she shared her story of forgiveness at a conference. Several people heard her story and felt God leading them to pay off her school loans. They discovered Helping Hands could help them give anonymously to someone in financial need, so they called Michelle.

Once Michelle contacted Shelby and qualified her as in financial need, she was able to make the gift paying off all of Shelby's student loans. Shelby was overwhelmed. God used a group of anonymous people to be the loving arms of her heavenly Father caring for her financial needs. This is the story of the joyful giver and the joyful recipient all in one.

God used a group of anonymous people to be
the loving arms of her heavenly Father.

AFTER A RESORT VACATION

Another favorite story is from a man we will call Sam. While Sam was on vacation, he felt God encouraging him to speak to one of the resort valets. He discovered that the valet's wife had lung cancer. She was receiving treatment, but it was miles away, so it was very difficult for them to arrange and pay for transportation.

Sam contacted Helping Hands because he heard they could give to individuals in financial need in a safe and secure manner. Helping Hands initiated a conversation with the valet and then arranged for Sam to anonymously donate for transportation so the valet's wife could easily get to her appointments. Although Sam didn't even really know the couple, he stepped forward to help a family in need.

A THOUSAND GIFTS

"There's a great joy in making a phone call to someone in need and telling them we have a grant for them from an anonymous donor," Michelle said.

There's the story of the young mom who transported several inner-city kids to school each day to make sure they would stay in school. Her car started breaking down and she began praying for a van so she could transport even more kids to school. A group of givers heard about her need and bought her a new van. She wept and jumped for joy at the same time when the new van was delivered to her.

"I truly believe generosity changes people," Michelle said. "Whether you're a believer or not, it's just a natural thing to thank God when your need has been met. Some pour their heart out in thanks even though they previously said they didn't really believe in God. Giving is transformative."

Debbie agreed, "This job has opened my eyes to a whole new world. There are still people in this day and time who enjoy helping others."

I truly believe generosity changes people.

Debbie's favorite part of her job is interacting with clients. In particular, she remembers a conversation with a gentlemen we will call Anthony. Anthony called Debbie one day to verify that one of his bills had been paid. In the process, he began sharing his story with Debbie: he and his wife both had cancer. He was doing better, but his wife was on life support in the hospital.

One day as Anthony was seeking the Lord for wisdom about what to do next, the verses the Lord gave him were Proverbs 3:5-6: "Trust in the Lord with all your heart, and do not lean on your own understanding. In all your ways acknowledge Him, and He will make straight your paths."

When Anthony went to the hospital later that day, a physician told him there was nothing more they could do to bring his wife back. He said, "Okay, Lord. You're being clear." Shortly afterward, one of his friends was getting pizza for Anthony and his children when he saw a vision of "tornados of angels" flying to Heaven, Anthony's wife among them.

Debbie was grateful Anthony shared his story with her, but she was shocked at the Proverbs verse he mentioned. That was the same verse the Lord had given her about a year before as she fruitlessly searched for a job after her middle-school-aged son sustained a traumatic brain injury playing football. He had to miss school for the rest of the year while needing around-the-clock care.

As Debbie shared her own story with Anthony and the verse's importance to her, Anthony said, "This phone call wasn't about me verifying a bill, but about you and me encouraging each other with Scripture."

Michelle added, "I am often amazed to discover how God gives grace to people in difficult circumstances right when they need it. They are often the most pleasant people you'll speak with. They're thankful, hopeful, and leaning on the mercy of God."

RESTORING THE JOY

Today, there are more than 1.5 million nonprofits in the country. There are hundreds of thousands of churches. In some cases, people have gotten a little fatigued with giving to an organization. Sometimes they just love the joy of being able to help someone directly.

James 1:27 tells us, "Religion that is pure and undefiled before God, the Father, is this: to visit orphans and widows in their affliction." That is the joy of Helping Hands. It is connecting the giver and the recipient. It makes the gift tangible because people get to see the impact of their gift. It looks like the following:

- The giver who made rent payments for the widow about to be evicted from her apartment.

- Hundreds of givers who paid for medical treatment for an eleven-year-old girl with a brain tumor and gave her a few more months with her family.

- A giver who paid for the tuition of an at-risk student and kept him off the streets.

- A couple's gift to help pay for the adoption of an orphan in a destitute land.

- An employee benevolent fund designed to help employees in financial need provided they also go through financial counseling.

There are more stories—a thousand more—but these are just a few of the stories of the generous givers and the joyful recipients.

YOUR STORY:

1. Think of two or three individuals who you know are in need. How might God be calling you to serve them? It may be financial assistance, or it may be as simple as a listening ear or a meal. Pray specifically for those individuals and be open to how God leads.

2. Sam was led to give after hearing the valet's story. This week, be intentional about truly listening to people, whether it is someone you know or someone you've just encountered in a coffee shop, airplane, restaurant, etc. What are their stories? Where are they rejoicing or struggling? Most of all, listen for opportunities to bless someone in a practical way.

3. Both Debbie and Anthony were blessed as they shared their stories of hardship and a verse that encouraged them during that time. How can you be open with your story to help others?

4. "My excess is likely someone else's necessity." This phrase is one that is often repeated at Helping Hands. What is your excess? Where could it be utilized to meet a greater need?

GENEROSITY

SUSAN PATTON
The Giving Circle (Nashville, TN)

CHAPTER 18

A WIDOW'S IDENTITY

"Happily ever after" isn't supposed to end with a plane crash—at least not when you've married your high school sweetheart at nineteen and your life is full as a wife and mother. A plane crash surely can't be the story that God writes for us, could it?

THE EARLY DREAMS

Susan has called Nashville, Tennessee home for almost all of her life, other than her college years in Memphis. Her growing-up years were not by any means perfect. Her parents went through a divorce when she was little, but still, life was stable. They were a lower middle-class family, but always seemed to have enough.

Like a lot of girls growing up, Susan dreamed of being a wife and a mother. At fifteen, she met Phil—and there were sparks right away. He was a year older, but they dated through high school and Phil was already displaying great traits of a future husband and business leader. He worked hard and life seemed to be on a good path. He graduated from high school and went to the University of Memphis and, one year later, Susan followed.

At college, Phil became a Christian and was discipled through Campus Crusade for Christ. Susan was intrigued by the changes in Phil but also shocked to realize there was life beyond what she'd experienced. She always thought her eternal destiny depended on her "goodness."

One weekend, she attended a retreat with Phil's church just so she could be with him. While there, one speaker discussed how the Holy Spirit draws people to Himself. The message was not explicitly evangelistic, but at that moment Susan realized, "Uh-oh. I'm being drawn." She said, "I could just feel it. It was just that kind of thing where you know God is tugging at your heart. It's not an emotional feeling; not a physical feeling; it's just a *feeling*. I realized I was on the outside and I was being drawn in."

With their newfound faith, Susan and Phil were married in 1973 at the ages of nineteen and twenty. Susan completed her nursing degree and worked for five years before their three children came along. At that time, Phil's work was going well, and she was blessed with the opportunity to stay at home with her kids.

As newlyweds, they went through a Larry Burkett financial study that taught them God owns it all, and they were just stewards of God's resources. This course reinforced Phil's desire to give. Although she didn't realize it at the time, this course would prove important in the years to come, even though Susan will tell you that her heart was not yet drawn to giving or finances. "That was Phil's area," she said.

LIVING THE DREAM

Some might have described them as the postcard couple. After his undergraduate degree, Phil pursued an MBA. After receiving his MBA in 1979, he joined HCA, one of the nation's largest for-profit hospital chains. He steadily rose through the ranks and by 1992 he was the senior vice president in charge of human resources. At home, Susan was blessed to raise her children—Ben, Elisabeth, and Julia. There were plenty of church and school activities to keep them all busy.

As they made more money, Phil would ask Susan what she thought about giving to this ministry or that, and she would agree. She said, "That was as far as it went with me. He was the one with the outside contacts in the business and ministry world. It's not that he didn't try to explain our finances to me, but I wasn't interested. I had my family. I had what I needed. And I knew we had more than enough money, so I was a happy camper."

But God was preparing Susan. As part of a church building campaign, the church asked them for what she considered a significant gift. She wrestled with it even though they appeared to have enough money and even some in savings. Yet Susan struggled as she wondered, "But what if we're going to need that money?" As they prayed together, God brought them peace to make this big gift.

THE DEATH OF A DREAM

By 2003, life was busy and full. Susan had managed to keep her nursing license active by taking continuing education classes and volunteering at camps and at a primary care clinic for the uninsured. At home, Susan's children were transitioning to college and young adult life.

And Phil was busier than ever. He served as an elder in the church, board member of the church school, board member of the local Salvation Army, and a volunteer at Siloam Family Health Center. In addition to these activities, Phil took up flying and purchased a Piper Saratoga with his brother.

But one day in October 2003, Phil went for a brief flight in the Piper. By the afternoon, he failed to show up for an appointment and a search team went out. The next morning, rescuers discovered the wreckage of his plane in a rugged stretch of Tennessee woods. The cause of the crash was unknown and inexplicable.

"Foggy, emotional, and shaky," are how Susan describes those first years following Phil's death. Most of all, there were the questions: "What are You doing, God? Why did You leave me in charge of all this?"

Now, nearly ten years after Phil's death, Susan said, "On this side of it, I've learned grief and questioning is very normal. And I'm not done—I'll probably grieve until the day I die. While I can't fully say I'm to the point where I'm glad it happened, it has strengthened my faith so I can tell God, 'You know I love You. I will love You, I will trust You no matter what.' God truly is my husband now."

LEARNING TO DREAM AGAIN

As the fog lifted, Susan had to redefine her identity. Her social life had revolved around church and her husband's work; that instantly changed when she was no longer one half of a couple. Most of all, she had to discover who she was before Phil because he had been part of her life since she was fifteen. "I started to dig into who I was before 'I' was 'we.' I could have made my children my identity, but they were in college and not settled yet. And that wouldn't have been right. It took a lot of trial and error, but I kept asking myself where my heart was. That's how I arrived back at nursing because I always enjoyed that."

I started to dig into who I was before "I" was "we."

Aside from reshaping her identity, Phil's death also left Susan in charge of everything. The financial aspect was especially daunting because she had never managed money before, never even balanced a checkbook. She knew they were well off, but did not realize by how much.

Also, about ten years prior, Phil had opened a private family foundation. Within days and weeks of his death, Susan began receiving requests. Promised monthly donations were becoming due. Ministries were submitting grant requests. Charity representatives wanted to meet with her.

In a meeting with her financial advisor, Susan broke down in tears when he asked her how it was going: "I haven't a clue about how to give money!" All she knew how to do was write the check and give the same amounts Phil had. However, she knew this would not be sufficient long term. After that meeting, her advisor began looking for events where Susan could learn about giving.

I haven't a clue about how to give money!

At one such event, a women's giving seminar, Susan heard about giving circles for the first time. She realized she was not the only woman at this stage in her giving or the only woman who would lose her husband. "My heart began to soften toward the whole thing," she said. "I think I was just so burdened by generosity at first: 'God, You must have made a big mistake here. You couldn't have possibly meant to leave me in charge of all this.' But I knew He didn't make mistakes, so I was just trying to learn that lesson."

Susan and a friend met with a woman who started a giving circle in Tucson to brainstorm and ask questions. Over the next eight months, they prayed about starting their own circle in Nashville. In the end, Susan and three other friends invited ten women to go through the Crown Financial Ministries Special Edition study. After the study ended, they asked the women if they would like to join the giving circle.

Today, the circle has fifty women. Each pays a membership fee of $600 a year (which is $50 a month). That money is then pooled and distributed to charities that have submitted an application after being recommended by one of the women in the circle.

Currently, the circle has distributed over $134,000 to Christian ministries in the last four years. "It is such a joy to see the other ladies get involved in giving," Susan said. "Many of them say it has opened up the topic of generosity with their husbands and families. And it blesses me to know that something good can come from something tragic."

Susan still occasionally struggles as she wonders if she is too open about her generosity. "I'm the type of person that I don't want to broadcast that I'm being generous," she said. "However, I have to trust that the giv-ing circle is God's leading. It's not, 'Look what I'm doing; here's what I want you to do,' but instead, 'Let's put all our money together—it'll make a bigger difference than what we could do separately—and in the mean-time, let's learn about new ministries and volunteer some places.'"

Susan believes generosity has made her life richer and fuller, and soft-ened her heart toward God and His work. "I've gone from being burdened by giving to seeing it as a great blessing. At first I felt like a bank—just giving out checks. But now God shows me who He wants me to support. Giving used to be a foreign language, but now it's my primary concern other than my family."

> At first I felt like a bank—just giving out checks.
> But now God shows me who
> He wants me to support.

Susan illustrates her viewpoint with a story about one of her friends who used to teach PE in elementary school. "One day this teacher told a student to run a lap and the student asked, 'Do I have to?' She said, 'No, you get to. See that boy in the wheelchair over there? He can't run, but you get to.'"

This is not a story Susan would have written for herself—from wife and mother, to widow, to giver—but she realizes now that her illustration is true: "Although it is a huge responsibility, I feel like giving is a 'get to' situation. It is a privilege to join God in His Kingdom work."

YOUR STORY:

1. When Susan was asked to donate to her church's building fund, she wrestled with the fear of the unknown and the fear of not having enough. Regardless of your financial situation, this is a common struggle. What are specific truths or Bible verses you could focus on in these situations? (One of Susan's favorite verses is 2 Corinthians 8:7.)

2. After Phil's death, Susan had to rediscover who she was again—and she eventually found it in nursing and generosity. When your identity or expectations for the future unravel, what are some ways you can find your heart again? Where have you found it?

3. Susan has gradually transitioned from seeing generosity as a burden to something she gets to do. How might God be calling you to view or practice generosity differently?

PERSISTENT GENEROSITY

And let us not grow weary of doing good, for in due season we will reap, if we do not give up. So then, as we have opportunity, let us do good to everyone, and especially to those who are of the household of faith.

—GALATIANS 6:9-10

MATT MCPHERSON

Mathews, Inc.; McPherson Guitars
(Sparta, WI)

CHAPTER 19

THIS GUITAR-PLAYING ARCHER RUNS

"Young man, run for Jesus; don't walk." More than twenty years ago, a stranger, an old man spoke these words to young Matt McPherson. They were words of confirmation for Matt as he pursued the vision God had for him. Today, Matt is still running—literally. He owns one of the largest archery bow companies in the world, builds custom guitars, leads worship with his wife, records CDs at his recording studio, and promotes "The Salvation Poem" internationally.

SOLID ROOTS AND A PROMISE

Matt was the second oldest of seven children, so his father, who owned an auto body shop, had to work hard to provide. In order to provide meat for the family, Matt's father began bow hunting (the bow was chosen because Matt's mother had a fear of guns). As soon as he was old enough, Matt also learned to hunt, an activity that would later provide the basis for his business.

Growing up, Matt's father was a good role model. In particular, he remembered when a company his father worked for asked him to falsify some information. Matt's father refused at the expense of losing his job. Through examples like that, Matt learned early on that the bottom line isn't about making money; it's about making the right decisions. He said, "I realized it's pretty simple: you never do what you want to do unless it's what you should do."

In high school, Matt's family struggled financially. In order to get by, he and his older brother often worked forty to sixty hours a week. While Matt would have loved to play high school sports, he said, "We learned early on to die to ourselves and what we wanted to do. I also realized I couldn't let myself get tied up in what I couldn't do."

Matt came to know Christ at an early age and continued to seek Him. He told God, "I'm not really interested in being important; I just want to do what's important." In 1977, the nineteen-year-old was praying and asking what God wanted for his life. God responded— audibly—and said, "I am going to prosper you in business so you can be self-sufficient in ministry." Matt was thrilled. "Okay, You want me to be a businessman. You know I'm not a very good beggar and I love to give."

However, it was still a journey toward that future. After high school, Matt, who had always hated school, joined his dad's auto body shop before starting his own. In his spare time, he studied metallurgy and engineering for fun.

In 1980, he married Sherry, the pianist for a Christian music group where he played guitar. (And more than thirty years later, they are still leading worship together and recording CDs with their record company, Autumn Records.) However, those first years of newlywed life were difficult financially. With interest rates of more than 21 percent in the early 80s, hardly anyone was buying new cars, which meant there were few used cars for Matt's auto body business.

Visions of Archery Bows

Gradually, Matt began sensing God was moving him toward the archery business. He had been building his own bows for a while and thought he could make it into a business. It was 1983 and he was still looking for God's promise of business prosperity, made six years earlier, to come true. While walking around the house one day, he clearly heard God say, "I know every answer to every problem in the world. If men would only ask Me, I'd give them those answers."

> I know every answer to every problem in the world. If men would only ask Me, I'd give them those answers.

Matt fell to his knees and said, "God, I feel You're calling me into archery and being a businessman. Because You know how to make better archery bows, I'm asking You for that wisdom. Direct me in a way that's unique and novel so I can build the best bows in the world, and I'll honor You with my life."

About two weeks later, Matt woke up in the middle of the night to a vision of a new bow design. "It was literally like a sheet of notebook paper. And that's what was funny—it wasn't just a white sheet of paper, but it was notebook paper hanging in my face." It took two more years to develop the concept, and then he started McPherson Archery in 1985 with the help of some investors. Later, he sold his controlling interest in 1987 and the rest of it in 1989 because the investors wanted to go in a different direction.

In the fall of 1991, he was driving when he had a vision for the single cam bow. In 1992, he started Mathews, Inc. with one employee. The business just exploded as this innovative new design provided the quietest and most accurate bows on the market. From 1992 to 1997, in the span of about five years, Mathews went from the smallest bow company in the world to an Inc. 500 company.

Within a few months of opening his business, he was able to pay off all his seed capital so he solely owned the company. He explained, "My wife and I wanted the freedom to support missions and give without an investor pressuring us to reinvest everything back into the company."

STAYING BUSY

Matt has continued to expand his business ideas. These include the National Archery in Schools Program (NASP), the fastest-growing PE curriculum in the nation; CenterShot, an archery program for churches; Mission Crossbow, for missions; and Lost Camo, a camouflage pattern company that gives all its profits to missions. Matt and his dad also started McPherson Guitars, whose quality, innovative guitars are frequently used in both the country and Christian music circles.

Matt said, "We have a unique situation where we can branch out into new areas as God continues to bless things. We're just going to take this to its conceivable height, all for the purpose of making more money to impact this world. We have over seven hundred missionaries worldwide whom we fully support. We really look for opportunities and are actively praying, 'God, open the doors so we can be more effective for You.'"

When people ask Matt how he can stay so busy, he said, "We know there will be plenty of time to rest in Heaven. The Bible says Heaven is better than we can imagine. And if Heaven is better than I can imagine—and I'm an inventor with over fifty patents—then you want to be there. I often challenge Christians with this: if I could send you to Hell for five minutes—really go to Hell for five minutes—and then send you to Heaven for five minutes, would you live your life the same? When I'm dying, I'm not going to be wishing I'd bought myself something else. I'm going to be thinking, 'I wish I would have done more for Christ.'"

When mentoring people, especially young adults, Matt often finds that people say, "Well…I'm trying! I screwed up because it's just so hard. But I really am trying." In response, Matt asks, "Are you trying like you're on fire?

Are you trying that hard? If your ability only gets you to nine percent, but you're truly trying like you're on fire, God will happily pick up the remaining ninety-one percent. All He wants to know is that you're fully in."

A WORLD-CHANGING IDEA

A few years ago Matt prayed, "God, making bows and guitars is wonderful, but could I have an idea that would change the world?" Immediately God replied, "Okay, I want you to write a sinner's prayer in poem form, set it to music, and teach it to the world." Matt thought, "Oh, my goodness. This is like 'Mary Had a Little Lamb.' I can't forget those words. No one can."

> God, making bows and guitars is wonderful, but could I have an idea that would change the world?

God continued, "Most Christians don't share Christ for a number of reasons, but for one, they're uncomfortable with the process. So if kids could learn a simple sinner's prayer, and it's as simple as sharing the 'Mary Had a Little Lamb' poem, how many more people would accept Christ?"

Matt wrote the song in a few minutes. He was stuck on the fifth line, but his wife, who is also a songwriter and poet, filled it in. It's a simple six-line poem on a durable card with supporting scriptural references on the back along with a place to write your name and the date you accepted Christ:

Jesus, You died upon a cross
And rose again to save the lost
Forgive me now of all my sin
Come be my Savior, Lord, and Friend
Change my life and make it new
And help me, Lord, to live for You
—THE SALVATION POEM

Today, the poem is on over 50 million pieces of literature worldwide in multiple languages. Its website, TheSalvationPoem.com, tracks the poem's impact. "This is probably the most important thing I'll ever be a part of," Matt said.

CRISIS

In December 2012, Matt got shingles, Lyme's Disease, and the flu all at the same time. He lost forty-two pounds as his body started shutting down and stopped producing the necessary chemicals a healthy body creates. It was so bad he was afraid he might be dying. But by far, the worst was the darkness. He said, "I went into a black, living death. I was super quiet and nothing brought me joy. And for the first time in my life, I couldn't hear God. I just felt dread and darkness. I would literally take walks in the dead of winter to try to connect with God, but very little happened. Never having existed would be better than this."

For the next few months, all Matt could do was read the Bible, pray, listen to praise and worship music, and try to talk to God. For a long time, he couldn't feel God at all. Gradually, however, he realized, "Hey, if I live my life by how I feel, this is not a good thing. I need to make sure I don't believe in God because I feel Him, but because of who I know Him to be."

After Matt began getting well, he realized this is what God wants us to do—to live by faith instead of feelings. He said, "When I went to a place that felt like Hell—in the sense of the dread, the horror, and the feeling that I was separated forever—what kept me together was what I knew. You could take away what I felt, but you couldn't take away who I knew God to be. He promised in His Word to never leave or forsake me."

You could take away what I felt, but you
couldn't take away who I knew God to be.

GIVING THOUGHTS

As far as giving goes, Matt has a lot to manage as he gives from company profits and from various nonprofits he runs. However, he believes in making wise investments. "It is easy to take money and throw it recklessly at ministries instead of saying, 'God, is this really the most effective place to put it?' Unless God specifically tells you to support a project, I always err on the side of choosing something that will be the most effective for the Kingdom."

Matt also enjoys hearing the stories of people affected by his giving. He said, "Even if you can't go [visit a ministry], be sure to request stories. When you start looking at real lives and real children who are changed by what you're doing, you want to do more. Also, you become more focused on the things that matter."

In spite of all this, Matt ultimately realizes that he is not necessary: "God really doesn't need me," he said. "His success does not depend on me. Once you know His success does not hinge on you, but that God would love for you to be a part of what He's doing, then working for Christ becomes a privilege."

YOUR STORY:

1. God told Matt, "I know every answer to every problem in the world. If men would only ask Me, I'd give them those answers." What answers are you looking for and where are you looking for them? How might knowing those answers help guide more people into the Kingdom?

2. If you could literally go to Hell for five minutes, and then to Heaven for five minutes, would you live your life the same as you are living it now? How would you live your life differently? What is keeping you from making those changes so you can live differently now?

3. For several months, Matt went through a very dark place where he could not connect with or feel God. Have you ever been in a similar place? What are some promises you can hold on to during those times?

DON CAMPION
Banyan Air Service
(Ft. Lauderdale, FL)

CHAPTER 20

RETURN TO EGBE

It's amazing how the experiences of childhood never leave you. Instead, they shape you, sometimes inspire you, and even call you back home.

Don Campion grew up as a missionary kid in Nigeria. His parents served at Egbe Hospital, a SIM (Serving in Mission) project in the Nigerian bush. Life was primitive. Communication was by short-wave radio, and the missionaries had to generate their own electricity, dig wells, and build their homes and furniture by hand.

Starting in first grade, Don was flown to a boarding school three hours away (a two-day trip overland). Three months later, the plane would return Don for a month with his parents. While the plane rides brought separation from his parents, they also inspired Don's interest in aviation.

After Don graduated from high school, he worked for World Vision for a year before attending aviation school in Toronto. He then moved to Miami, Florida, where he began flying chartered airplanes to the Bahamas. He even met his wife, Sueanne, at the airport where she would frequent those flights.

As Don flew, he began to notice the company owners were having difficulty maintaining the airplanes in their fleet. He asked if he could service the aircraft he was flying along with any others that needed maintenance—a question that would become the start of his company. In 1979, the twenty-five-year-old Don rented a hangar at Fort Lauderdale Executive Airport, named his company Banyan Air Service, and began maintaining numerous aircrafts.

Over the years, God has blessed the company. Today, Banyan has over one hundred eighty employees, known as teammates, and is recognized as one of the top five business aviation companies of its kind nationwide. They cater to private and corporate turboprop and jet aircraft and offer twenty-four-hour fuel service, ground support, aircraft sales, comprehensive maintenance, avionics installations, aircraft parts sales, a retail pilot shop, and a restaurant.

BUSINESS AS MINISTRY

While Don knew God was part of his business, it was not until 2000 that he began to understand how his business was his ministry. "When you dedicate your life to Christ," Don said, "God doesn't call you to *the* ministry, but to *a* ministry. And my ministry is excellence in aviation. Christian businessmen who truly believe they are stewards of a business God owns should be pursuing excellence and trying to become the best at what they do."

God doesn't call you to **the** ministry, but to **a** ministry.

As part of that ministry, Banyan seeks to invest in each teammate from the day they arrive. Not only are they encouraged to become better workers, but better people, spouses, and parents. To achieve these ends, Banyan provides a wellness program, a fitness trainer, an in-house gym only for teammates, personal finance tutoring, numerous training programs, and a corporate chaplain who is available on-site every Thursday and by phone all the time.

Banyan also has a Spirit Committee that chooses community engagement projects. This committee chose to support 4Kids of South Florida, a Christian foster care organization that runs ten homes for children waiting for placement. Banyan adopts a home and maintains it with new carpet, drywall, paint, light fixtures, and anything else it needs.

Don carries his mindset of doing excellent work into the ministry world. "As a business guy, you understand what it takes to run a successful company. I challenge you to get involved with a ministry at a grassroots level. Some business guys may say they don't know how their work is ministry. That's nuts! Go pick a ministry and learn about their accounting, their leadership, their problems, and their goals. Help them in their board meetings. Understand what the impact could be if they were more efficient and successful. What's their strategy? How can you pray for them? Those are all things business owners can do in their sleep."

RETURN TO EGBE

God wasn't done with Don and his company, however. In 2008, Don innocently took his wife to Nigeria to show her where he grew up. When he got there, Egbe Hospital was nothing like his childhood memories. No SIM missionaries had lived there for over five years and SIM had turned the hospital over to a local church. Because of a lack of leadership and an insufficiently trained staff, the hospital had deteriorated to a clinic at best. It appeared on the verge of extinction.

When he returned to the States, the fate of Egbe Hospital nagged at the edge of his consciousness. Finally, Don wrote a letter summarizing the problem: for over half a century, this hundred-bed hospital served thousands of people and represented years of missionary sacrifice. Instead of starting a new hospital, shouldn't this hospital be revitalized?

Don sent the letter to SIM first, but told them he would present Egbe to other organizations if SIM did not want the project. In 2009, a SIM discovery team investigated the hospital and came back excited. Led by Don, they crafted a five-year plan to revitalize Egbe Hospital. By June of 2010, the Egbe Hospital Revitalization Project was an official SIM endeavor. In 2011, a partnership was finalized with Franklin Graham and Samaritan's Purse, bringing teams of roofers, plumbers, backhoe operators, electricians, and more to Egbe every two weeks.

Unbeknownst to Don, his teammates at Banyan decided to support the hospital project. Now, when Don goes to Nigeria for several weeks in March, August, and November, he always brings volunteers from Banyan who come for two weeks and donate their time by not requesting overtime pay or travel reimbursements. Through their business contacts, Banyan is also able to ship three forty-foot containers every year full of top-quality medical and construction equipment that is proven to withstand use in the tropics.

Through the hospital project, Don has clearly seen God's hand at work, from moving shipping containers into the country trouble-free, to arranging a meeting with a Nigerian state governor and ministers of health, to having the national Nigerian telephone company offer to install a cell phone tower with Internet right on the hospital grounds, and much more.

Don said, "If God is really our Master and Savior, why do we limit Him so much? That is the lesson we've learned so clearly. God is the source of all wealth and He's given it to us to glorify Him by financing Kingdom investments. If you are investing in something that's the Lord's will, why would He let it run out? The original five-year plan to resurrect the hospital is peanuts compared to what's actually happening—surgeons, nurses, and doctors from the States are moving to Egbe and it will be so much bigger, better, more efficient, more advanced, and more comfortable now."

> God is the source of all wealth and He's given it to us
> to glorify Him by financing Kingdom investments.

Don recognizes that the success of this endeavor does not depend on him. Before they get involved in any project, they always send a prayer team ahead of them. Before proceeding with the Egbe project, they asked for prayer from all the churches within twenty miles of the hospital. Then they went to all the retired missionaries who had served within two hundred miles of the area. Today, there are probably five to six hundred people who pray for Egbe Hospital daily. For example, at a church a mile from the hospital, three hundred people gather six days a week at 4:30 a.m. to lift their hands toward the hospital and pray for it.

WHAT GOD HAS SHOWN

Originally, Don named his company "Banyan" because his accountant told him he needed to incorporate and think of a company name to file taxes. The name came from the banyan tree, an African tree with hundreds of roots that grow from the tree's branches into the ground and eventually thicken into trunks that are indistinguishable from the main trunk. Banyan trees are known to cover acres of ground and sometimes even entire villages are built beneath the hanging roots. Don realizes that Banyan has been an appropriate name for his company: through the providence of God, this company is growing large and providing shelter for others.

Don said, "We're really still in the middle of the adventure and I'm not just sitting here reflecting on it. We're halfway through a five-year plan and it's going to be ten times better than our original plan. Generosity, in my opinion, is about stepping out in faith and giving outside your comfort zone. It's about giving sacrificially as opposed to the leftovers or what you feel comfortable giving after you've lived the year you wanted or bought what you wanted."

He concluded, "God prospers you not to raise your standard of living, but your standard of giving. That's a neat way to think about it."

YOUR STORY:

1. Don said, "Christian businessmen who truly believe they are stewards of a business God owns should be pursuing excellence and trying to become the best at what they do." Why is it important to pursue excellence in your work? How have you seen excellent work open doors for more ministry opportunities?

2. Don challenged business owners to use their professional skills to get involved with a ministry. What skills or talents do you have? How could you use those to serve a ministry?

3. Prayer plays such an important role in starting and continuing on with the Egbe Hospital project. Who is on your prayer team or what people are you praying with? Next, think about where you work, live, play, or go to school. Are there people who live or interact in those places who might want to pray with you for that area?

4. Don said that in his opinion, generosity is about giving of your talents and stepping outside of your comfort zone to give sacrificially. Does generosity always include sacrifice? Why or why not?

GENEROSITY

JOHN AND SHERRI KASDORF
The Kaztex Foundation
(Pewaukee, WI)

CHAPTER 21

A JOURNEY OF SEVEN CAREERS

John Kasdorf describes himself as a maladjusted middle child who has gone through seven *career* (not just job) changes. "I got bored or got an itchiness to move on," he said. But now as John reviews his career path that ranges from military officer to energy consultant, he sees how each piece has led him deeper into the generosity journey. Today, the seventy-one-year-old John focuses on what he calls his "encore career"—running the family foundation with his wife, Sherri.

A FIRST INFLUENCE, LOVE, AND JOB

John grew up in Milwaukee, Wisconsin, surrounded by a strong family presence. Even today, all of his siblings and children still live in the area. Growing up, his family valued education and church. John's father, a lawyer, was the first in his family to get a college degree, and, continuing in that tradition, all of his children have obtained advanced degrees. Church attendance was also a non-negotiable due to the cultural expectations and religious discipline of the entrenched Lutheran and Catholic communities.

As he headed to college, John obtained an NROTC (Naval Reserve Officers) scholarship, so he spent his summers on "cruise training." One summer while on a cruise out of Subic Bay in the Philippines, John saw extreme poverty for the first time in his life. "I saw what the rest of the world looked like, how blessed I'd been, and how separated from the pain and suffering I'd been. I knew that at some point in my life, I needed to do something about it."

Several years into his naval career, John was transferred to Naples, Italy. One moonlit summer night at a senior officers' party, the lieutenant was captivated by a young woman—Sherri, the daughter of a career Navy officer from Beaumont, Texas. Sherri had lived in Hawaii and on both U.S. coasts before her father was transferred to Italy right after her high school graduation. She was a sophomore at Texas Christian University and had been living with her parents in Italy during the summers.

As summer ended, Sherri's parents, convinced this was only a summer romance, told Sherri to return to Texas for her junior year. Sherri only lasted a semester before returning to Italy in December. Six months later, in June 1969, John and Sherri were married.

After another six months in Italy, the Kasdorfs moved to Madison, Wisconsin, so they could finish their respective graduate and undergraduate degrees. Sherri taught elementary school for a few years before staying at home with their three sons.

John began working as a securities analyst at a mutual fund company. Within five years, he had been promoted and even had his own accounts. However, he began to get antsy. Aside from the factory line type of work, it was also a difficult time in the mid-70s: "I began to get frustrated because no matter how smart you were, when you decided something was a good investment, if the markets were down, the markets were down. I was depressed about how little influence I had in the world around me. I also felt a deep sense of responsibility and failure when we lost clients' money."

A NEW DIRECTION

A man who owned an investment advisory firm then offered John a job and ownership in the company. After interviewing over a six-month period, John quit his first job to take this new one. However, right before he started, Sherri was outside working in their yard when a messenger arrived with a telegram. "I wouldn't want to be getting this one," the messenger said. Sherri took the telegram to John: the man had changed his mind. Even before a day on the job, John was fired.

He was devastated. He said, "I was this person with all this world experience and education. I thought I was a pretty energetic guy ready to make things happen, and all of a sudden, I'm out on the street." And not to mention, Sherri was pregnant with their first child.

Eventually, John was interviewed by a headhunter who directed him to his next job as a corporate consultant at Hewitt Associates, an actuarial firm. At Hewitt, he specialized in consulting on investments for retirement plans. He said, "I was never interested in being an actuary, but over time God showed me how much I loved consulting and helping people find their own solutions. It was a fascinating utilization of my instincts because, instead of trying to benefit myself with my skills, I was helping others."

Five years later, he struck out on his own to continue his investment consulting. As he built his business, he began meeting with oil and gas entrepreneurs and eventually put together about fifty partnerships for energy projects. He said, "The definition of "expert" is a guy who knows a little bit more than the guy next to him. So the fact that I knew how to spell energy, and how it came out of the ground, and how to invest in it without all the fingers in the middle of it in New York, meant I had a distinct competitive advantage."

As energy projects in general fell apart in the 80s, John knew he needed to reinvent himself or become a different type of entrepreneur. He started an energy management business that purchased natural gas for companies. He said, "That career exploded and turned out to be the business that has funded our family foundation. When we sold it in 2003, we were the third largest purchaser of natural gas in the state of Wisconsin."

A Tension from Childhood

Through this journey, John and Sherri have needed to discuss what generosity means. John said, "I think it's been a tension all my life. My grandfather, who was a very competent business executive, was reduced to selling eggs and life insurance to survive during the Depression. And because I grew up with Depression-era parents, everything had to be reused. Everything I had was a hand-me-down from my brother. It was never mine. Also, there was an attitude of fend-for-yourself. I had an older brother, so I was constantly getting elbowed out by a stronger kid."

In fact, for John's eighth grade graduation, he asked for his own suit of clothes. It was the first time he wore something nice that was his own. "So whatever the opposite of sharing is, that was impressed on me," John said.

The other tension came from tithing. "At the church I grew up in, you felt obligated to give a certain amount every Sunday as the plate went by," John said. "Not that I object to that, but it just seemed counterintuitive to be putting money in the plate and at the same time knowing I had to go back to the house and fight for 'my share' of things. That's been a tension I still work on today."

Sherri also had Depression-era parents. Her mother sewed all of Sherri's clothing until Sherri rebelled against that in high school. When she turned fourteen, she got a job (even though she was underage) just so she could buy store-bought clothes.

THE DEAL

When John and Sherri's children were young, John watched the offering plate go by one Sunday. He thought, "I put money in this envelope every week just like I always have. But what is this all about?" He was frustrated that there seemed to be no plan or explanation for how the gifts were used. So he made a deal with God: "I'm going to become more engaged and intentional by giving a specific percentage of my prior year's taxable income—the tithing concept. But I'm going to start cheap, maybe two percent, and see if this tithing thing works or not."

> I'm going to start cheap, maybe 2 percent,
> and see if this tithing thing works or not.

While John cannot remember what he asked for in return, he wanted to see if he could resolve the tension between feeling like he had to grab for everything and, on the other hand, giving in a disciplined, generous way. "Of course, regardless of how our giving grew over time, God always provided," he said.

Another influential moment came when they received a request from a local rescue mission—for $1.75 they could provide a family with Thanksgiving dinner. At the time, the Kasdorfs had two small children and very little money. Sherri said, "We talked about it and decided yes, we could do this. We could feed a family. So we wrote a twenty-five dollar check. It was so tiny, but it was one of the first gifts we gave as a couple. It's all these little things in the beginning that started our generosity journey." Today, Sherri is on the board of that same rescue mission and they still send out the same cards on Thanksgiving.

John's view on generosity took another freeing turn when he heard a conference speaker, Bill Eisner Sr., explain how he used his business for Kingdom work. Whenever Bill was not using his printers for his advertising business, he was using them to print Christian material. John said,

"Before, I figured you weren't a full Christian until you were in ministry. I'm just a business guy who can't get myself out of the marketplace because that's what attracts me. So I see a guy who is also a business junkie except he is also doing Kingdom work with it. All of a sudden, I saw what a privately-held, Christian company could look like."

> I'm just a business guy who can't
> get myself out of the marketplace
> because that's what attracts me.

LESSONS ON FAMILY GIVING

In the mid-1990s, the Kasdorfs used the proceeds from their energy management company to start a family foundation so they could be more intentional with their giving. Reflecting their desire for legacy and generosity, the foundation's principles are 1) helping people in need, 2) in southeast Wisconsin (local focus), and 3) sharing Christ.

The Kasdorfs have also found their giving is often personality-driven. For example, the foundation has both a nonprofit and for-profit side. The for-profit helps the nonprofit remain sustainable while also giving John an outlet to experiment with new business ideas. Because John is a hands-on entrepreneur, he enjoys looking for needs that are not being met. On the other hand, Sherri is extremely relational—she is a caretaker and shepherd.

Despite their differences, John said, "Our marriage has been extremely critical in our growth in generosity. We complement each other in this area. I'm the idea guy and very conceptual. I've got all these ideas for what we could do with these resources—I'm leading with the vision, direction, and finances—but Sherri's leading with her time and talents. On weeknights, she has taken groups to the rescue mission to work with the women. I realized that this is what the whole picture looks like—we need to bring it together as a family."

And as far as their family goes, John and Sherri are still figuring out how to pass on a legacy of generosity and to more fully invite their children and grandchildren into it. "Maybe we weren't ready to, but if I look back at it, maybe we could have started earlier with our kids and done better," John said. "We did service projects together, gave them money to give away, and did some training on finances, but we certainly could have done more. But we're fortunate they still live in the area and all of our sons work within the context of our foundation in varying capacities."

As they consider their generosity journey, John said, "We're humbled to bring up the conversations, but we are not the experts on this. Whatever has happened has been to the glory of God and not to us."

YOUR STORY:

1. Both John and Sherri wrestled with generosity after growing up with the tension of Depression-era parents. How did your childhood affect your views on generosity? What good lessons from the past can you put into practice? What old fears or emotions need to be laid aside so you can live generously?

2. Not every generosity journey begins with a colossal moment of inspiration: much of the Kasdorfs' growth came in little steps like giving 2 percent to church or writing a $25 check. What next little step might you be called to take? Or, when you look back, what little things has God used to guide your own journey?

3. John and Sherri have very different personalities, especially when it comes to giving, but this actually benefits them as they begin to see generosity holistically. How is God using your spouse's view of generosity to grow both of you? What can you learn from your spouse?

GENEROSITY RESOURCES

ACCEPTABLE GIFT

www.acceptablegift.org

Acceptable Gift presents living and giving from God's perspective. They offer books and resources that serve churches, nonprofits, and individuals at all income and wealth levels.

COMPANIES WITH A MISSION

www.cwam.com

This nationwide initiative encourages and rewards volunteers from the workplace who come together to serve charities and have an impact in their communities. Winning teams receive a share of more than $1 million for their charities.

COMPASS: FINANCES GOD'S WAY

www.compassl.org

Compass is a worldwide interdenominational ministry that teaches people of all ages how to handle money based on the principles of the Bible.

CROWN FINANCIAL MINISTRIES

www.crown.org

Crown Financial Ministries equips servant leaders, churches, and individuals to live by God's design for their finances, work, and life.

GENEROUS GIVING

www.generousgiving.org

Generous Giving provides generosity retreats, an annual event, and giver stories to encourage people in their own generosity journey.

GENEROUS LIFE

www.generouslife.com

Generous Life is a consulting firm that helps affluent families create a lasting legacy by ensuring they know their story and have a well-defined set of values, a clear vision, and a practical mission.

GLOBAL GENEROSITY MOVEMENT

www.generositymovement.org

The Global Generosity Network collaborates with Christian churches, alliances, networks, business leaders, professional networks, workplace fellowships, and generosity ministries to encourage Christian giving and stewardship.

HALFTIME

www.halftime.org

Halftime works with mid-life marketplace leaders who desire to live the second half of their life rich in eternal significance.

HELPING HANDS MINISTRIES

www.hhmin.org

Helpings Hands provides direct financial assistance to deserving and qualified individuals, ministries, and charities.

iDONATE

www.idonate.com

iDonate offers marketing support and helps ministries receive and process all donation types, including non-cash gifts.

I LIKE GIVING

www.ilikegiving.com

I Like Giving is a nonprofit created to inspire a generous world. Its website serves as a platform for unique storytelling and idea sharing that wants your action and story, not your money.

KINGDOM ADVISORS

www.kingdomadvisors.org

Kingdom Advisors is a community of Christian financial professionals integrating faith and practice for Kingdom impact.

MAXIMUM GENEROSITY—BRIAN KLUTH

www.kluth.org

Brian Kluth provides resources, sermons, cartoons, and books on biblical stewardship, giving, tithing, and fundraising.

NATIONAL CHRISTIAN FOUNDATION

www.nationalchristian.com

NCF is the largest Christian grant-making foundation in the world. They work with givers, ministries, and churches to create a culture of generosity.

ONE HUNDRED SHARES

www.onehundredshares.org

One Hundred Shares is an Atlanta-based nonprofit that supports local ministries. They also provide support and tools to women seeking to start their own giving circles.

WOMEN DOING WELL

www.womendoingwell.com

Women Doing Well inspires a movement of generous living for women by helping them discover their unique gifts and giving them the necessary tools to manage all that has been entrusted to them.

ABOUT THE AUTHORS

WILLIAM F. HIGH is the Chief Executive Officer of National Christian Foundation Heartland where he is a sought-after leader and speaker on generosity and family legacy. He works with families, individual givers, and financial advisors to help facilitate God's call to generosity. He specializes in coaching affluent families and their advisors on the transference of holistic wealth to heirs. Bill is a visionary leader energized by people and ideas, and, as a former lawyer, the law taught him how to ask great questions to find the truth.

Formerly, he was a partner with the law firm Blackwell Sanders Peper Martin, LLP and he remains Of Counsel with Sanders Warren & Russell, LLP. He is also the founder of iDonate.com, Generous Life, FamilyArc, and Christian Foundation Grants. His aim is to change the paradigm by which people think about generosity and to make generosity generational.

William holds a B.S. in education from the University of Missouri-Columbia and a J.D. from the University of Kansas School of Law. He has been married to Brooke since 1987 and they have two daughters and two sons.

ASHLEY B. MCCAULEY is the marketing and editing coordinator for Generous Life and FamilyArc. She has a Bachelor of Arts degree in communications and biblical studies from Moody Bible Institute. She previously interned with Moody Publishers and also enjoys freelance writing, editing, and blogging. Ashley's goal is to help others tell their stories, discover hope, and believe their true identity in Christ. She is married to the love of her life, Ben.